AN INTERACTIVE

JOURNEY

GUIDE THROUGH

WITH

THE HOLY LAND

JESUS

BOB GOFF

A JOURNEY WITH JESUS
Published by David C Cook
4050 Lee Vance Drive
Colorado Springs, CO 80918 U.S.A.

A Ministry of Cook Media Global

Integrity Music Limited, a Division of David C Cook
Brighton, East Sussex BN1 2RE, England

ISBN 978-0-8307-9129-3
eISBN 978-0-8307-9130-9

The author is represented by Alive Literary Agency, www.aliveliterary.com.

The Team: Michael Covington, Stephanie Bennett, Jeff Gerke, Judy Gillispie, Karissa Silvers, Susan Murdock
Cover Design: Leah Von Fange

Printed in the United States of America
First Edition 2026

1 2 3 4 5 6 7 8 9 10

110725

CONTENTS

GREETING FROM BOB

Hi there!

Have you ever been on a grand adventure? Maybe you've traveled the world to see or do something amazing. Possibly you took a hike in the woods as a child, and your imagination transformed it into a harrowing journey where you saved a friend from grave danger. You may have jumped out of a plane, gone scuba diving with sharks, or tried something new at your favorite restaurant. Whether you've laced up your hiking boots and climbed Kilimanjaro or thrown some helmets on your kids and whizzed around on bicycles through your neighborhood, you know that any type of adventure stirs up excitement, puts your skills to the test, and requires a bit of your time and focus.

That's what we're really doing here together: allowing ourselves to get caught up in God's grand adventure through the Holy Land by giving Him our expectation, rapt attention, and unique talents.

I wish I could buy everyone a plane ticket to physically come with me on this adventure. All the way to Tel Aviv, I'd talk to you about my wife, Sweet Maria, our wonderful grandkids, and the giraffes that are going in at the Love Does Restore University in Uganda. Unfortunately, there isn't a plane big enough to carry us all. So I came up with an idea that was the next best thing: Write a not-so-typical Bible study! In these pages, we can immerse ourselves in the very places we read about in Scripture, discover where God has moved throughout history, and find out how He continues to direct us today.

Most of our personal growth happens outside our comfort zone, and we bless our communities most by actively serving and stirring up good. That's why God wants us to go on grand adventures like these: so He can blow the lid off the box of what we thought He was capable of and bring people into our lives who make us better. So, where are you right now? Where is God taking you? If you're ready for an adventure, let's turn the page and find out!

Sincerely,
Your Travel Guide,
Bob

HOW THE STOPS WORK

All are invited to join this ride. You can be a theology student, a tire-shop employee, or a Bible study group full of people from all walks of life. You can enjoy this book on your own, with a partner, or with a group. You can even do this study alone first and then invite some friends to join you and do it a second time. Everyone is welcome on this trip because God has a beautiful, whimsical, and wild plan for us all. To really get our spiritual juices flowing and jump into the locations we'll visit, you'll find introspective questions, fun activities, and group discussion prompts. Allow God to use this book to guide you through the Holy Land as both He and you see fit. Here are a few tools and handy reference points you'll discover along the way:

- **Map:** At the beginning of each stop, you'll find a map that shows where we're going and just how far we've come. Feel free to make fun notes or doodles about both physical and personal landmarks or anything else you want to remember along the way.

- **Videos:** At each stop, you'll find a video that allows you to visit that place in the Holy Land with me. We'll experience the sights, sounds, and atmosphere, and we'll learn cool historical and theological details about it. You can watch alone or with friends. Choose your journey and let's go!
- **Find Your Friends:** Have you ever used the Find My Friends app on your iPhone? It's an app that allows you to share your location in real time with other people. In this Bible study, the Find Your Friends section asks you to do the same—pause for a moment and see what you can share with others about what God is teaching you on your journey in real time. Shift from a "me" mindset to a "we" one, and use these sections to guide group discussions and spark ideas for taking the message into the world around you.
- **Read Your Map:** In these sections, we're talking about the road map for every Christian's life: the Bible. Here, we'll read what God's Word has to say about the places, events, and people we'll be learning about on our trip.
- **Drop a Pin:** Just as you might drop a pin on your phone to share your location, in these sections you're going to pause and take a good look at where you are on this journey. Take this space to reflect and get honest with God, yourself, and your group so you can keep moving in the direction you want to go.
- **Personal Travel Log:** At the end of each section, you'll find space to write or sketch about what you've learned at each stop. Dig deep. Write a few notes or a prayer. This is *your* log, so create it how you feel led to best document the adventure God takes you on.
- **Extend Your Stay:** If you're just not ready to leave yet, scan the QR code and you'll find more relevant (and fun) information for each stop. Get in on the action! Visit the links provided to explore live webcams or other fascinating videos from some of these historic spots. Take a moment to see what I saw, and put yourself into the dusty, holy, magnificent places around the Holy Land.
- **Recipes:** At the end of each stop, I'll share one of my favorite recipes from each location. Try these with your Bible study group, and eat together before or after your gathering, cook with your family and share what you've learned, or get creative and enjoy on your own. Nothing puts you into these sites like experiencing

them with your senses. While the videos provide the visuals, these recipes will bring in the delicious aromas and tastes of different parts of the Holy Land. (You can also download each recipe by scanning the QR code.)

A note about Scripture citations: The Bible quotations in this study are generally taken from the New International Version (NIV) of the Bible. As the most widely used Bible translation in the world, it is the easiest for us all to understand. However, you are more than welcome to look up any of these passages in your favorite translation.

Now ... let's get started!

Capernaum

STOP 1

INVITING EVERYONE INTO COMMUNITY IN CAPERNAUM

Bob's Travel Log

The first stop on our trip is Capernaum. It's remarkable to be in the central location Jesus used for His ministry. I mean, Jesus walked, taught, and performed miracles right here in this town! I can almost see Him strolling on the northern shore of the Sea of Galilee behind me and calling out to two fishermen, Peter and Andrew, as they cast their nets. "Come, follow Me!" Jesus shouted. And guess what? They dropped their nets and became fishers of men. I wonder if that discarded net is buried under centuries of sand somewhere close by.

Since Capernaum is a former trading center, there are ancient ruins everywhere. We will explore the remains of synagogues, the site thought to be Peter's house, and other archaeological sites around the village. Even before we get started on this trip, I can feel a sense of serenity in the beach air. It's like you can tell that Jesus touched this place and its people, making Capernaum live up to its name: a joining of the word *caper* (meaning "village") and the name *Nahum* (meaning "rest").[1]

There are layers upon layers of evidence that Jesus made an incredible impact on this place, and I'm excited to see how He changes our lives on this trip too. Let's go!

It's time to watch the video for this lesson.
Settle in for a few minutes and scan the QR code (access code: Journey).

In the video, I'm sitting in the location of Peter's mother-in-law's house. That's amazing, isn't it? Walking in the footsteps of the people we read about in Scripture really makes the Bible come to life. I want to shout, "What? I can't believe it. This is all real!"

I hope God gives you several of these "aha moments" on this journey through the Holy Land. I hope He blows your socks off as we discover together where we're at in life and where God may be taking us. So, before we keep going, let's pause (always a good idea on a long trip) and reflect.

Drop a Pin

- **Where are you right now in relation to what I spoke about in this section's video? Excited? Curious? Lost? Jot down your thoughts in the space below.**

FINDING MORE THAN TREE-LEVEL FAITH

Read Your Map

> They came to Bethsaida, and some people brought a blind man and begged Jesus to touch him. He took the blind man by the hand and led him outside the village. When he had spit on the man's eyes and put his hands on him, Jesus asked, "Do you see anything?"
>
> He looked up and said, "I see people; they look like trees walking around."
>
> Once more Jesus put his hands on the man's eyes. Then his eyes were opened, his sight was restored, and he saw everything clearly. Jesus sent him home, saying, "Don't even go into the village." (Mark 8:22–26)

As we begin our tour, let's think about this story of the blind man in the city of Bethsaida (near Capernaum). In ancient times, blindness would have made this man's life very difficult. This man couldn't fish like all his neighbors. He couldn't work the land to farm and provide food. He would have been fully reliant on others. Maybe he was a beggar. On top of this, his culture associated sickness and blindness with sin. People believed that hardship was punishment from God. This blind man was an outcast.

But he wasn't without support. When news reached Bethsaida that a healer and prophet named Jesus was in town, some friends scooped up the blind man and led him to Jesus.

I want friends like that, don't you? I need people in my life who, when they see me hurting, don't leave me or judge me but get me closer to Jesus. Friends can hold us, but only Jesus can heal us.

- **Take a moment to identify a few of the friends who hold you until Jesus heals you.**

Group Discussion Prompt

Look back at Mark 8:23 and fill in the blank:

He took the blind man ____________
____
and led him ___________________
______________________________.

Don't you love this detail? Jesus didn't make this suffering man a spectacle. He gently led him somewhere private to minister to him.

If you were the blind man, you would have felt Jesus' hand guiding you and heard the crunch of gravel under your feet as He led you out of the village. You might've questioned your hearing—and Jesus' methods—when you heard Him spit and put His hands on you. I'm sure you would've been shocked. You might have been equally astonished when Jesus asked you, "Do you see anything?" and you did!

- Has Jesus ever surprised you? Have His ways shocked you? In those times, what did He do?

- Have you ever been caught off guard by a friend giving you an incredible gift or a stranger doing something nice for you? What happened?

- Take another look at Mark 8:24. How did the blind man respond to Jesus? What did he see at first?

• Now write down any names that come to mind of friends who will bring you closer to Jesus. (If you can't think of any right now, that's okay! Write down a description of a friend you would like to have.)

Every time I've read this, I've wondered what reference this man had for trees. Maybe he had seen trees before as a child and lost his sight later in life. Who knows? What we do know is that after Jesus' first touch he could see some but not completely. He could've lied and told Jesus, "Yay! I can see!" and moved on. He had the option to accept only partial sight and say, "Good enough. This is so much better than what I had." But he didn't. He was honest, and that led Jesus to offer him a second touch.

• Look at the end of our passage in Mark 8. After Jesus put His hands on the man's eyes a second time, what happened?

It's as if the blind man had enough faith in Jesus to get him halfway there, but when he literally started to see that Jesus could heal, his faith needle jumped to the max. He was ready for a full healing on that second try.

- **What do you have only tree-level faith about right now?**

- **What do you think might be holding you back from fully believing that God will come through?**

Reflecting on this man's story of healing leads us to questions we must ask ourselves: Are we being real with Jesus? Are we telling Him what we actually need? Let's be honest for a minute.

- **In the space below, write down what you want to ask Jesus for (guidance, healing, hope, relief from anxiety and depression, something for your children or a family member ... anything at all!).**

- **Now jot down any areas where you need a "second touch" from Jesus. Maybe cancer has returned, your finances are going downhill again, you're revisiting that addiction, you've explored different religions but now you're ready for a relationship with Jesus, or you feel called to petition God again with a prayer you'd given up on. Let it out in the space below, because what we see in Mark 8 is that Jesus doesn't mind honesty and a second ask.**

Drop a Pin

- **To see where you're at right now in life, answer the question that Jesus asked the blind man: Do you see anything? In your relationships, thought patterns, and environment, what do you notice is going on? Is there any area where you can see God at work in your life? What is He doing? Jot down your thoughts in the space below.**

IF A DOOR DOESN'T OPEN, TEAR OFF THE ROOF

Read Your Map

> One day Jesus was teaching, and Pharisees and teachers of the law were sitting there. They had come from every village of Galilee and from Judea and Jerusalem. And the power of the Lord was with Jesus to heal the sick. Some men came carrying a paralyzed man on a mat and tried to take him into the house to lay him before Jesus. When they could not find a way to do this because of the crowd, they went up on the roof and lowered him on his mat through the tiles into the middle of the crowd, right in front of Jesus.
>
> When Jesus saw their faith, he said, "Friend, your sins are forgiven." (Luke 5:17–20)

The Capernaum/Bethsaida area must've had numerous suffering people, because we again see a disadvantaged man who was brought to Jesus by his companions. Lives were dramatically impacted by good friendships!

In our previous story, the blind man seemed to encounter Jesus outside. But in Luke 5 the paralyzed man faced the obstacle of a crowd surrounding Jesus in a house.

It doesn't take much investigating at these ancient sites to realize that a home in biblical times would have been a simple stone-and-mud-brick structure. Homes were small too. There was no giant living room for a crowd to gather in or a big backyard where people could pull up a lawn chair to hear Jesus teach. The crowd on this day would have been spilling out of the tiny home into the courtyard.

This could have discouraged the paralyzed man's friends. As soon as they realized it was going to be nearly impossible to push their friend and his mat through the crowd to get into the house, they could have said, "Oh, well, God closed the door," and justified not trying any harder. But they didn't.

While the walls of a home in Capernaum were pretty solid, the ceilings were not. They were made mostly of straw and dirt. So this man's friends decided that if the door was closed, they'd just have to tear off the roof.

That's sometimes the path for us, as well: If a door doesn't open, maybe you should tear off the roof.

Jesus, in the middle of His message, must have felt dirt hitting His face. Straw would have fallen and become tangled in His hair. As He looked up, He would have seen not only a paralyzed man descending through the torn ceiling but also the determined and desperate faces of the man's friends.

Sometimes I think we give up too easily. We look at the obstacles in our path and say, "Oh, well, God closed that door." But what if He wants us to tear off the roof? What if this is our opportunity to activate something in our lives or the lives of others and do something about what we need?

- **In the space below, write about a time you gave up on something too early.**

- **Are you tempted to give up on something right now?**

- **What might it look like for you to tear off the roof and get creative about activating an answer to your prayer?**

Discuss your ideas with the group.

Find Your Friends

Look back at Luke 5:20 and fill in the blanks.

When Jesus saw ____________________________________ faith, he said, "____, your sins are forgiven."

When Jesus saw *whose* faith? Not the faith of the paralyzed man but the faith of his friends. Can you believe that? We have so much power as friends! We can be the ones to lower someone in front of Jesus, and He will move in their lives because of the actions we took on their behalf.

As I shared in the video, the best way I've found to lower somebody in front of Jesus is just to be available to them. You don't have to preach at people or come up with some crazy way to get them to come to church with you. You don't have to have all the answers to their questions. Just become a safe place for someone. Have meaningful conversations.

- **Identify someone or a few people in your life you can carry to Jesus; write their name(s) in the space below.**

Here are a few ideas for meaningful conversation starters (you can also use the video for reference). Fill in the blank lines with your own questions.

- What was it like to grow up being you?
- What were the stories you made up to explain why life is sometimes complicated or painful?
- What are the rules you made up then that you still live by today?

____

____

____

Jesus Christ has made every believer a new creation. He is taking us on a terrific adventure of walking as new creations. And the thing about being a new creation is that you have to do stuff differently, because, as I say, "If you just keep doing the same thing, there ain't nothing new about that." And no one displayed this better than the disciples.

Drop a Pin

- **Has there ever been a time when you had to help carry a friend through a hard season? Has anyone had to support you as you healed? What happened? What impact did it have on your life? Discuss your answers with the group.**

Group Discussion Prompt

If you're doing this Bible study with a group, you can start talking about these questions with each other. Also, you can go back through the list of names you just wrote down and start building trust and having meaningful and powerful discussions.

- Look up 2 Corinthians 5:17 in your Bible and write down what it says.

PUT DOWN YOUR NETS; PICK UP NEW LIFE

Read Your Map

> As Jesus was walking beside the Sea of Galilee, he saw two brothers, Simon called Peter and his brother Andrew. They were casting a net into the lake, for they were fishermen. "Come, follow me," Jesus said, "and I will send you out to fish for people." At once they left their nets and followed him.
>
> Going on from there, he saw two other brothers, James son of Zebedee and his brother John. They were in a boat with their father Zebedee, preparing their nets. Jesus called them, and immediately they left the boat and their father and followed him. (Matt. 4:18–22)

It's wild that in a split-second decision, Peter and Andrew went from fishermen to fishers of men. They became entirely new creations the moment they decided to follow Jesus. And the same thing happens to us.

Look at our Scripture again and fill in the blanks:

> ____________________ they left their nets and ____________________ him.... Jesus called them, and ____________________ the boat and their father and ____________________ him. (vv. 20, 22)

These disciples reveal that we are radically in charge of our lives and decisions. This means that you and I too can immediately decide to drop our nets (all those lackluster things we have been chasing in life, like success and money and careers and earthly satisfaction) and begin to pick up hope, love, grace, faith, and wonder. We can go from moving in one direction to pivoting toward Jesus and never looking back.

- **What nets have you been carrying that are weighing you down?**

- **What do you think it would look like for you to set them aside and make the radical decision to start following Jesus?**

Now, following Jesus is going to take some determination. I'm sure these men had their doubts and questions. They didn't even fully know who Jesus was yet, after all. However, they decided to take this journey with Jesus just one step at a time. And that's what we're doing here today: walking with Jesus one step at a time. Through Capernaum and beyond.

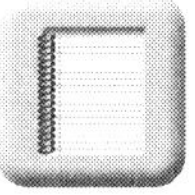

Personal Travel Log

Reach deep. In Capernaum, God is calling us into being honest with Him. He's calling us into healing relationships with friends. And He's calling us into new life by urging us to let go of our old habits. As you reflect on all you have learned, consider these questions:

- **Where do you see yourself in relation to these Scriptures? Do you need to be carried by friends right now? Do you need to pick up someone else's mat and bring them to Jesus? What net do you need to cast aside to pick up all that God has for you?**

- **Where do you see God at work in your life and in the lives of others around you?**

- **What is God calling you to do in light of our time in Capernaum?**

- **What direction do you think He wants you to go next?**

Pray

Jesus,

You are the One who opens every blind eye. I don't want to settle for "tree-level faith"; I want the fullness of what You have to offer. Will You please offer me a second touch in the areas where I need it?

Thank You for the friends who carry me to You when I can't walk. Teach me to be that kind of friend too. May my faith help someone else find the healing and hope they need.

If, like the disciples, I need to leave something behind, please help me have the faith to let it go so I can walk freely in You.

You've already met me here in this journey—through Bethsaida, Capernaum, and the pages of Your Word. Now send me forward—changed, honest, healed, and ready.

Amen.

Extend Your Stay

If you want to spend a little more time at this stop, scan the QR code here (access code: Journey). You can take a tour through Capernaum, download a digital recipe, and find cool links.

Recipe

St. Peter's Fish

Located close to the Sea of Galilee, Capernaum—the city Jesus used as His headquarters and where He called former fishermen to become His disciples—has for centuries been known for seafood, particularly fish.

The fish popular in Capernaum is commonly known as tilapia, but it's no surprise that over time this town adopted a new name for it: St. Peter's fish. Traditionally, the tilapia is either grilled or fried and served with tahini or garlic sauce and a side of lemon.

To really experience all the flavor of this seaside city, try cooking St. Peter's fish in your own home or with your Bible study group. Here's an easy recipe.

YOU WILL NEED:

2 tablespoons garlic powder
2 tablespoons salt
1 tablespoon pepper
2 tablespoons paprika
½ stick of melted butter, or 2 tablespoons olive oil
4 tilapia fillets
1 lemon, cut into wedges
fresh parsley
tahini

DIRECTIONS:

1. Mix together all the spices and set aside. Warm the butter or oil in a skillet over medium heat.
2. Once the liquid is warmed, add tilapia and cover generously with the spice mixture.
3. Cook the fish on each side for 2–3 minutes or until cooked through.

4. Set the fillets on a plate, and squeeze lemon juice over them.
5. Garnish with parsley, and serve with tahini and an extra lemon slice.

If you're looking for a few sides, St. Peter's Fish is tasty served with rice and veggies.*

*Based on a recipe from https://faithmag.com/st-peters-fish-pronto.

The Valley of the
Shadow of Death

STOP 2

PAVING A PATH OF PROTECTION IN THE VALLEY OF THE SHADOW OF DEATH

Bob's Travel Log

Welcome to the valley of the shadow of death! We're overlooking a steep valley some miles east of Jerusalem, and if you take a turn to the south, you'll head toward the Dead Sea. This valley is deep, surrounded by steep, rocky slopes, which helps us understand why King David might have been referring to this place when he spoke of "the valley of the shadow of death" in Psalm 23:4 (NKJV). David fled here when King Saul's jealousy drove him to chase David into the wilderness so he could try to find him and kill him. This valley was his path into the wilderness.

I'm certain he felt overshadowed here, both in body and soul. Ironically, this is also the valley where David claimed victory over his fears (see Ps. 23). Sometimes when we're in the darkest places, God's light shines brightest, doesn't it?

Another valley we'll visit is the Kidron Valley, which begins on the eastern edge of Jerusalem, sloping dramatically between the Temple Mount and the Mount of Olives, and extends toward the Judean desert and the Dead Sea. From where I stood, I could see the giant stones of the temple, olive trees stretching their branches through the dry Middle Eastern air, and white limestone tombs dotting the hillsides.

Everything there served as proof that the things in the Bible really did happen. Some of those tombs belong to biblical characters like Absalom and Zechariah. Idols were burned there during the reforms in 1 Kings. According to John 18, Jesus walked through this very valley with His disciples on His way to the garden of Gethsemane to pray before His crucifixion and resurrection.

Both of these valleys served historically as gateways from hurt and hardship to hope and healing. I'm praying they still lead us there today. On the other side of the darkest valley is always life in Jesus, so let's head on through!

It's time to watch the video for this stop.
Settle in for a few minutes and scan the QR code (access code: Journey).

I have a confession: Before we filmed that video, we hiked down into the valley, and I almost fell. It made me really grateful for my guides and team, because they were there to correct my steps and show me the way forward.

As I read Psalm 23, I thought about when I tripped, and it made me thankful for God's "rod and staff," as David put it (v. 4). I could just picture myself as a sheep in a flock trying to cross some of these cliffs, and I could imagine a shepherd holding out his rod saying, "Whoa there, Nelly! Back up so you don't fall and get hurt." God too is there to help guide us forward when we aren't certain of our next step. He offers us sure footing because we can count on Him. He knows the way! Before we keep going, let's pause and reflect.

Drop a Pin

- **Where are you right now in relation to what I spoke about in this section's video? Excited? Curious? Lost? Jot down your thoughts in the space below.**

WHEN YOU'RE IN PAIN, KNOW THAT GOD'S PRESENCE IS PROMISED

Read Your Map

Your hands have made me and fashioned me,
An intricate unity;
Yet You would destroy me.
Remember, I pray, that You have made me like clay.
And will You turn me into dust again?
Did You not pour me out like milk,
And curdle me like cheese,
Clothe me with skin and flesh,
And knit me together with bones and sinews?
You have granted me life and favor,
And Your care has preserved my spirit.

And these things You have hidden in Your heart;
I know that this was with You:
If I sin, then You mark me,
And will not acquit me of my iniquity.
If I am wicked, woe to me;
Even if I am righteous, I cannot lift up my head.
I am full of disgrace;
See my misery!
If my head is exalted,
You hunt me like a fierce lion,
And again You show Yourself awesome against me.
You renew Your witnesses against me,
And increase Your indignation toward me;
Changes and war are ever with me.

Why then have You brought me out of the womb?
Oh, that I had perished and no eye had seen me!
I would have been as though I had not been.
I would have been carried from the womb to the grave.
Are not my days few?
Cease! Leave me alone, that I may take a little comfort,
Before I go to the place from which I shall not return,
To the land of darkness and the shadow of death,
A land as dark as darkness itself,
As the shadow of death, without any order,
Where even the light is like darkness. (Job 10:8–22 NKJV)

Some theologians argue that the valley of the shadow of death is more of a metaphor than a literal place because some form of this phrase is used by various authors throughout the Bible (e.g., Job 3:5; Ps. 44:19). We can all agree that this valley represents the dark, dangerous, hopeless places that we've all wandered through in life. The valley of the shadow of death is the lowest of low points where we're surrounded by towering problems and often think God has forgotten about us in the messy middle. Kind of like Job.

- **What did you gather about Job from the passage we just read? How does he describe the valley of the shadow of death near the end of the passage?**

If we back way up in the book of Job, we find out that he was a pretty awesome guy. Take a look at Job 1:1 (NKJV) and fill in the blanks:

> There was a man in the land of Uz, whose name was Job; and that man was ____________________ and ____________________, and ____ and __________________________.

Sounds like the definition of a great, godly man, right? As we dive further into the book, we find that because Job is so good and so in love with God, Satan wants to see if he can break his spirit. However, God knows Job is a man of integrity, and He gives Satan permission to test him. In just a few short chapters, Job's children, wealth, and health are all taken away. He is left on an ash heap, crying out to God.

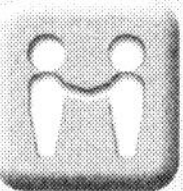

Find Your Friends

Have you ever offered someone bad advice? I know I have. My super-enthusiastic, love-driven personality can sometimes lead me to spout off tips or encouragement before I fully understand someone's situation. I genuinely want to be helpful, but

I've learned over time that true kindness often involves asking more questions and offering a listening ear or a shoulder to cry on rather than just having the right answers.

I think this is how Job's friends felt. If you look at their conversations from Job 2–31, you notice that they want good things for their friend Job, yet they offer him some bad advice. They believe Job must be hiding some secret sin that is causing his suffering. So they say things like:

> Who, being innocent, has ever perished? (4:7)
> When your children sinned against him, he gave them over to the penalty of their sin. (8:4)

While we do know that there are consequences to our sin, we also know that sin wasn't the cause of Job's problems. His friends didn't ask him the right questions. They didn't keep sitting with him in his suffering. They just pointed fingers and tried to offer him a solution.

- **If you've ever offered someone bad advice, what happened? What do you think it looks like to do this well, to offer a friend good insight and help them when times are tough? Who is someone you can trust to sit with you in your suffering?**

Job's friends weren't the only ones giving him bad advice.

- **Read Job 2:10 and write down how Job answered his wife when she told him to "curse God and die" (v. 9) in the space below:**

I wish I could say I would have responded the same way in his situation, don't you? But when things are taken away from us that hold value, it's tempting to curse God and ask why. Like kids when one of their siblings takes away their toy, we want to scream, "That's not fair! Give it back!"

Back when I was just starting my law firm, Sweet Maria and I bought an old Victorian home, complete with a walk-in vault. We were young and building a bank account, so we didn't have much to put in there except for a few things that were personally valuable to us, like Pop-Tarts and our kids' favorite toys. However, if I'd had something of great value, you'd better believe I would have locked it up in that vault. I would have been angry if someone had broken into that vault and stolen something extremely valuable to me.

- **Have you ever felt that something of great value was unfairly taken from you? What was it? How did that affect your view of God?**

In his valley of the shadow of death, Job learned a skill that we all could benefit from. When Job had everything taken away from him, he realized that he could be honest about his questions and pain but also count on God's presence to remain. He was able to accept whatever life threw at him because he counted his relationship with God, not his possessions or even his relationships with people, as the ultimate prize. As a result, even in his doubt and lament (which is just a fancy word for an expression of grief), God showed up.

- **Take the time to read God's conversation with Job in chapters 40–41. Why do you think God responded to Job in this way?**

Group Discussion Prompt

The valley of the shadow of death is a hard place to be. I mean, you can tell that just from its name. The life of Job is evidence that righteousness doesn't guarantee a life free of hardship, and we are allowed to weep and wail about that. We can be honest with God about our pain. We can trust that He will not only hear us but also be with us. Now, bad things will unfortunately happen because we are broken people who live in a broken world full of other broken people. However, from bad things, God will always work something good and in line with His purposes for those who follow Him.

- Are you in a valley of the shadow of death right now? What do you need to be honest with God about regarding your situation? What is keeping you from trusting in His ability to do something good with a bad circumstance?
- If you're doing this Bible study with a group, answer some of these questions together. If you feel led, take time to pray over each other's circumstances and ask God to make good of the bad.

Most of the book of Job makes us ask the age-old question "Why do bad things happen to good people?" As honorary consul for the Republic of Uganda, I've been highly involved in human rights work, especially for kids who are wrongly imprisoned. These children are innocent! Why would God allow such bad things to happen to them?

In my capacity as honorary consul and throughout my life, I've had to ask myself, *Will I trust in my knowledge and understanding or in God's surpassing wisdom? Will I lean solely on my power, or will I trust that God can move mountains, pick us up out of the valley of the shadow of death, and give great purpose to suffering?*

Read the following verses and write down how God's presence shows up in our pain.

- Isaiah 55:9

- John 16:33

- Romans 8:28

- Ephesians 3:20–21

- Philippians 4:4–6

Job reveals to us that if we allow God to lead us through the valley of the shadow of death, His restoration and blessing await us on the other side (though not always in the ways we expect). So continue trusting God in both the good and the bad, and keep going!

Drop a Pin

- **In the space below, write or doodle about what suffering you or a loved one is experiencing that goes beyond your understanding. What is hard about having faith in God when you're stuck in the middle of a dark valley? Feel free to discuss with your group or a close friend.**

A ROUGH ROAD CAN LEAD TO RESTORATION

Read Your Map

A messenger came and told David, "The hearts of the people of Israel are with Absalom."

Then David said to all his officials who were with him in Jerusalem, "Come! We must flee, or none of us will escape from Absalom. We must leave immediately, or he will move quickly to overtake us and bring ruin on us and put the city to the sword."

The king's officials answered him, "Your servants are ready to do whatever our lord the king chooses."

The king set out, with his entire household following him; but he left ten concubines to take care of the palace. So the king set out, with all the people following him, and they halted at the edge of the city. All his men marched past him, along with all the Kerethites and Pelethites; and all the six hundred Gittites who had accompanied him from Gath marched before the king....

> The whole countryside wept aloud as all the people passed by. The king also crossed the Kidron Valley, and all the people moved on toward the wilderness. (2 Sam. 15:13–18, 23)

As David sorrowfully crossed the Kidron Valley, he may have been reminded of his earlier psalm. Let's look at his story to see why he might have written a song of such heartache and hope.

It might be a dead giveaway with all the shepherding analogies in Psalm 23, but David started out as a shepherd boy. He spent most of his young adult years tending to sheep in a field and fending off predators like lions and bears. The day-to-day grind was probably pretty humble and mundane. Sheep are known as some of the most vulnerable and panic-prone animals on the planet, so David would have been constantly steering them in the right direction and keeping them out of harm's way.

In the middle of one of these normal days as a shepherd boy, things started to change dramatically for David.

- **Take a moment to read 1 Samuel 16. What happened? How did David end up in the service of King Saul?**

Isn't it amazing how David goes from ignored to anointed? Can you imagine what it would have been like to move from a pasture into a palace? David's life is truly fascinating, and I recommend reading his whole story or listening to 1 and 2 Samuel using a Bible app the next time you're in the car on a trip. It's a wild ride. But if I had to summarize David's life up until we get to our key Scripture in this section of 2 Samuel 15, it'd go like this:

David served King Saul as a musician for a while until he slayed a giant named Goliath in a war between the Israelites and the Philistines, which made him a national war hero. He did this in his everyday clothes with just a sling and a stone, a weapon he would have been highly trained with as a shepherd. This stunned all of Israel. As a result, King Saul welcomed David into his court and even gave him one of his daughters in marriage. However, as David's fame grew, so did

Saul's jealousy of the young leader, and Saul ultimately decided to kill David. This sent both of them into the wilderness for years, with Saul chasing David and David hiding from Saul.

Through the time David spent as an outcast, he learned to truly trust in God. God provided all he needed, including an army. That ragtag group of outlaws stuck with David (gaining the most awesome nickname of David's "mighty men" [2 Sam. 23:8 NKJV]) until Saul was eventually killed in battle and David finally ascended to Israel's throne. He conquered lands, united Israel, and achieved too many military victories to count.

This all happened right around the areas we are visiting in the Holy Land! However, David's story wasn't a fairy tale. It's documented in the Bible, so you know there were some hardships and obstacles that came David's way.

- **Read 2 Samuel 11:1–5. What did David do? Why was it a sin?**

- **Now look at 2 Samuel 12:10–14. What were the consequences of David's actions?**

Find Your Friends

Nathan was a prophet at the time of David's reign as king. He was also one of David's spiritual advisers. In 2 Samuel, we see that David and Nathan's relationship was one of both trust and truth. Even when it was hard, Nathan chose to hold David accountable in a way that he knew David would receive. So he told David a parable (a short story with a moral or spiritual lesson), called his friend out, and helped him pivot back toward God's plan for his life.

I have a few Nathans in my life too. These friends aren't impressed by anything I've done, and they're not scared to call me out when I get offtrack. The truth is that we all need people in our lives who don't always agree with us. We need people who remind us of who God created us to be. I'm so grateful for these friends who keep me focused on loving others and living out my purpose. It's also a great honor when I get to be that person for someone else.

- **Take a moment to think of a few people in your life you trust to speak the truth when you need to hear it. Write down their names and thank God for them. If no one comes to mind, that's okay! Write down a few names of people you may want to ask to hold you accountable.**

Read 2 Samuel 19:14 and fill in the blank:

> He won over the hearts of the men of Judah so that they were all of one mind. They sent word to the king, "________________________, you and all your men."

In his darkest valley, David faced curses, hardship, hunger, and grief over the loss of his son. Yet he remained faithful to God, prayed strategically, and trusted the Lord to restore his kingdom. Ultimately, David and his people walked back through the Kidron Valley into a restored Israel.

David's journeys through both the figurative and literal valleys are evidence that wilderness seasons don't always turn out to be worst-case scenarios. When we trust God with our lives, keep ourselves surrounded by true friends we can trust, and keep moving in the right direction, rough roads can lead to restoration. We may not inherit a literal kingdom like David did; however, God does give us access to His kingdom, presence, and love. It's a hard but fruitful decision to walk through the valley of the shadow of death with the light and love of Christ rather than by your own abilities. That is why David concluded Psalm 23 with "Surely your goodness and love will follow me all the days of my life, and I will dwell in the house of the LORD forever" (v. 6).

So find some friends and keep moving forward. Goodness and love are always on the way!

Drop a Pin

- **What has God taught you through David's adventure through the valley of the shadow of death?**

- **Where are you right now—in the middle of the valley, on the other side in the wilderness, or back on restored land?**

- **What does it mean to you that God's goodness and radical love are following you no matter where life takes you?**

Group Discussion Prompt

What does it look like to serve our friends by speaking the truth in love, as Nathan did? How do we become a safe place, build trust, and call others up into who God made them to be? Remember, this is correction and even discipline or rebuke that you or someone else is bringing. What does our attitude need to be when someone does this for us?

When God tells David (through Nathan), "Out of your own household I am going to bring calamity on you" (2 Sam. 12:11), it doesn't sound good, does it? And it isn't. After David loses his first son, several of his sons try to murder each other and take their father's throne.

This brings us to 2 Samuel 15 and our encounter with David's son Absalom. He's handsome and uses his charisma to charm the people in Israel and start a rebellion. This sends David and his followers on the run for their lives and straight into the Kidron Valley, or the valley of the shadow of death.

- Take another look at 2 Samuel 15:23. Where are David and his followers headed toward on the other side of the valley?

- Hop over to 2 Samuel 18:9–17. Read what happened to Absalom and write down any details that stand out to you.

THE DARKNESS DOESN'T LAST FOREVER

Read Your Map

When he had finished praying, Jesus left with his disciples and crossed the Kidron Valley. On the other side there was a garden, and he and his disciples went into it.

Now Judas, who betrayed him, knew the place, because Jesus had often met there with his disciples. So Judas came to the garden, guiding a detachment of soldiers and some officials from the chief priests and the Pharisees. They were carrying torches, lanterns and weapons.

Jesus, knowing all that was going to happen to him, went out and asked them, "Who is it you want?"

"Jesus of Nazareth," they replied.

"I am he," Jesus said. (And Judas the traitor was standing there with them.) When Jesus said, "I am he," they drew back and fell to the ground.

Again he asked them, "Who is it you want?"

"Jesus of Nazareth," they said.

Jesus answered, "I told you that I am he. If you are looking for me, then let these men go." This happened so that the words he had spoken would be fulfilled: "I have not lost one of those you gave me."

Then Simon Peter, who had a sword, drew it and struck the high priest's servant, cutting off his right ear. (The servant's name was Malchus.)

Jesus commanded Peter, "Put your sword away! Shall I not drink the cup the Father has given me?"

Then the detachment of soldiers with its commander and the Jewish officials arrested Jesus. They bound him and brought him first to Annas, who was the father-in-law of Caiaphas, the high priest that year. Caiaphas was the one who had advised the Jewish leaders that it would be good if one man died for the people. (John 18:1–14)

As I'm sure you've picked up on by now, the Kidron Valley is a place of deep sorrow, suffering, and transition. Like David, Jesus was rejected as king and betrayed by someone He loved. Imagine, thousands of years had passed between David (Jesus' twenty-eight-times-great-grandfather, according to Matthew 1) and Jesus. But they both took steps through the rocky, rough, unforgiving landscape of the Kidron Valley to accomplish a similar purpose. After a time of great suffering, they both restored kingdoms and set people free. How cool is that?

Take a look at the statements below, and see if you can match them to either David or Jesus. Circle the right answer (find answers on p. 174). (I'll keep all the pronouns lowercase here so I don't give anything away!)

- Betrayed by his son (David/Jesus)
- Betrayed by Judas (David/Jesus)
- Prayed on the Mount of Olives in the garden of Gethsemane before his arrest (David/Jesus)
- Prayed on the Mount of Olives as he fled for the wilderness (David/Jesus)
- Returned to Jerusalem as king after winning a great battle (David/Jesus)
- Will one day return as the King of Kings (David/Jesus)
- Trusted God for restoration: "If I find favor in the LORD's eyes ..." (David/Jesus)
- Submitted to God's will: "Yet not my will, but yours be done" (David/Jesus)
- Had a great earthly kingdom (David/Jesus)
- Has an eternal kingdom and will reign forever (David/Jesus)

- **Take a moment and read Isaiah 9:2. Write down what this prophecy said that Jesus would accomplish for the people.**

- **Why do you think Isaiah used the imagery of light in the midst of darkness? How does this tie into our understanding of the valley of the shadow of death?**

When Jesus walked through the Kidron Valley, all of humanity had been living in great darkness since the fall in Eden. A Messiah had been promised to God's people, a Savior who would come to deliver them. But for four centuries after the return to Israel from Babylonian exile, God seemed to be quiet. There is a four-hundred-year gap between the last book of the Old Testament and the first book of the New Testament.

God was silent while the Jewish people were conquered first by Alexander the Great and then by the Roman Empire. Meanwhile, they continued to try to follow the law of Moses (which included the Ten Commandments and a whole bunch of other rules about how God wanted His people to live).

However, no matter what they tried or how sincere they were, they consistently fell short. When they would sin (by breaking one or more of those rules), they would be in a form of broken relationship with God. They could make things right with Him by bringing their best animals to the temple as a sacrifice.

I don't know about you, but I mess up a lot! Can you imagine the weight people carried because of their mistakes? Think about all the sacrifices they would have had to make. Life would have been hard and hopeless.

But finally, four centuries later, Jesus came on the scene, and it was like the lights started to come back on. God heard His people and began to speak again. Thousands witnessed Jesus' miracles and experienced healing. They heard His teachings and experienced the hope, joy, and freedom He offered to all who would believe in Him. Things were getting brighter. That's probably why the darkness tried one final time to snuff Jesus out.

- **Read Matthew 27:32–56. In your own words, what happened?**

It's interesting to note that verse 45 says, "From noon until three in the afternoon darkness came over all the land." Satan thought he had buried the Light of the World in darkness when Jesus was crucified on the cross. But take a look at what really occurred:

- **Read Luke 24:1–8. What happened to Jesus?**

- **Take a look at Acts 26:22–23. When Jesus rose from the dead, what message did He bring?**

- **Now read 2 Corinthians 4:6. Where does the light of Jesus now shine?**

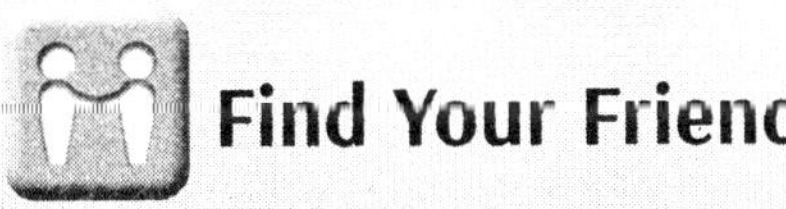

Find Your Friends

One of my favorite Bible passages is Matthew 5:14–16, which says,

> You are the light of the world.... Let your light shine before others, that they may see your good deeds and glorify your Father in heaven.

How awesome is it that we are the light of the world? We get to take all this joy, whimsy, and wonder found in the mystery of God and run with it into the darkness to make a difference in the world around us. What a wild and wonderful calling God has placed on all our lives. Take a moment to think about and answer the following questions:

- **Where might God be calling you to be a light to someone else walking in darkness?**

- **How can you live today as someone who has seen the great light?**

Personal Travel Log

Reach deep. In dark valleys, we get honest with God about how hard life can truly be. We also find out He's with us even in the lowest of lows. When we're in pain, we can cling to God's presence. When the road is rough, we can still hope for restoration. When times are dark, we can trust that our circumstances can't snuff out the light of Jesus burning inside of us.

- **What is your key takeaway from this section?**

- **Where do you see God at work in your life and in the lives of others around you?**

- **What is God calling you to do in light of our time in these two famous valleys?**

- **What direction do you think He wants you to go next?**

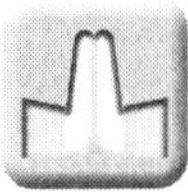

Pray

Father,

You see where I am, even when I'm deep in the valley. In the darkest places, You do not leave. You light the way.

Thank You for being the Shepherd who steadies my feet when the path feels rocky. Thank You for the rod that corrects and the staff that comforts, even when I can't see what's ahead.

Like Job, I've had times when I've questioned You and asked You why. I've wrestled with moments when life felt unfair. But I'm learning that I'm not walking this valley alone. You've walked it before me. You walk it beside me now.

Help me trust that Your presence is my protection, even when You don't remove the pain. Help me believe that restoration is still possible, even when the path is rough. Help me trust the Nathans you send my way who speak truth when I need it most.

When I wonder if the valley will ever end, remind me: You restore. You redeem. You resurrect.

Amen.

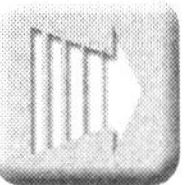

Extend Your Stay

If you want to spend a little more time at this stop, scan the QR code here (access code: Journey). You can tour the Kidron Valley, download a digital recipe, and find cool links.

Recipe

Maqluba

(UPSIDE-DOWN RICE WITH CHICKEN AND VEGETABLES)

Located in Jerusalem, the Kidron Valley region is known for a deep connection between food and faith. The recipes here are not only rich in flavor and full of earthy spices but also meant to be traditions shared with friends and family.

Because studying the Bible and gathering with your friends or family is a cause for celebration, I chose to share with you a recipe that the people of this area would also cook for a party: maqluba, or upside-down rice with chicken and vegetables. This dish is full of flavor and fun, and its preparation requires flipping over the pot it's cooked in, which is meant to be a crowd-pleasing event.

So invite your friends or Bible study group over, ask for some help in the kitchen, and gather around the table for maqluba before you dive into this week's material. Savor the flavor, community, and God's Word. It's bound to be a great celebration.

YOU WILL NEED:

2 eggplants, cut into small rounds
1 ⅔ cups basmati rice
8 boneless skinless chicken thighs
2 cups olive or sunflower oil, divided
1 onion, peeled and quartered
10 peppercorns
2 bay leaves
4 cups water
1 cauliflower, cut into florets
1 tablespoon butter, melted
4 tomatoes, sliced in ¼-inch wedges

8 cloves of garlic, peeled and halved

1 teaspoon ground turmeric

1 teaspoon ground cinnamon

1 teaspoon ground allspice

¼ teaspoon ground pepper

½ teaspoon crushed red pepper

1 teaspoon baharat (an all-purpose Middle Eastern spice that you can find at the grocery store or omit if you wish)

1 teaspoon salt, plus more for seasoning

Pine nuts, for serving (optional)

Herbed yogurt or cucumber sauce, for serving (optional)

Lemon wedges, for serving (optional)

DIRECTIONS:

1. Salt eggplant slices and leave on a paper towel for about 30 minutes to pull the moisture out of the fruit.
2. Rinse the rice and soak it in a bowl of water for 30 minutes.
3. Tenderize the chicken thighs with a mallet, and season both sides with salt and pepper. Heat 1 teaspoon of oil in a saucepan over high heat. Cook the chicken on both sides for about 4 minutes. Add onion, peppercorns, bay leaves, and water and bring to a boil. Then reduce heat to medium or medium-low. Simmer for about 20 minutes. Once the chicken is cooked, remove it and set aside before straining and reserving the broth.
4. Warm remaining oil in a Dutch oven over medium heat (the oil should be about ¾ inch deep). Cook cauliflower for about 5 minutes until browned. Then remove to a paper towel–lined plate and season with salt and pepper.
5. Pat the eggplant slices dry with paper towels. Repeat step 4 with the eggplant slices.
6. Discard the oil and wipe the pot clean. Cut parchment paper in a circle to fit the bottom of the Dutch oven to prevent sticking. Then brush the sides of the pot with melted butter. This will ensure the maqluba flip goes smoothly.

7. Now it's time to layer the maqluba. Arrange the tomatoes in an overlapping pattern. Next, arrange the eggplant in a layer. Then scatter the cauliflower. Add the cooked chicken thighs and finish with the rice and garlic on top. Press the rice down evenly.
8. Skim off any fat that has settled on the reserved chicken broth. Whisk in the turmeric, cinnamon, allspice, ground pepper, crushed red pepper, baharat, and salt, and gently pour the leftover chicken broth over the rice until covered. Press down on the rice if it seems too dry, until the broth covers the surface. If needed, add a little more liquid but just enough to cover the top of the rice.
9. It's finally time to cook! Heat the broth over medium heat until it begins to boil. Then reduce the heat to low and cover with a lid. Cook for 30 minutes, and then remove the lid and quickly cover the pot with a clean kitchen cloth. Replace the lid and allow the dish to sit for about 10 minutes.
10. Time to flip! Remove the lid and cloth and place a large serving dish over the toppot. Flip the pot and allow the maqluba to sit for 3 minutes. Then remove the pot in a grand presentation.
11. If desired, top with pine nuts and serve with cold herbed yogurt or cucumber sauce and a wedge of lemon.

Enjoy with friends and family. Remember, this is a celebration!*

*Based on a recipe from https://somethingnewfordinner.com/recipe/ottolenghis-maqluba.

Magdala

STOP 3

CARRYING A DEVOTED FAITH LIKE MARY IN MAGDALA

Bob's Travel Log

We're in the region of Galilee, the place where Jesus spent 80 percent of His ministry. It's awesome to think that Jesus might have stood on this very spot. Because Jesus spent most of His time in this area, we will too.

Off to my right is the former small, ancient Galilean fishing town of Magdala. Situated on the western shore of the Sea of Galilee, Magdala is small but beautiful. Stone paths run past ancient ruins like the foundations of villas with stunning mosaic floors, fish-processing pools, and *mikva'ot* (ritual purification baths), evidence that this was once home to a thriving Jewish population who truly lived in community.

"Magdala" comes from the Aramaic word *migdal*, which means "tower" or "fortress,"[1] possibly in reference to its cultural vitality as a fishing, trading, and shipbuilding hub.[2] The lake and this location, towered over by the jagged cliffs of Mount Arbel, take your breath away. You can just picture fishermen docking and chatting while salting their catch, Jesus sharing a parable in the synagogue, and Mary of Magdala (or Mary Magdalene) returning to her hometown with the disciples, tears filling her eyes as she witnesses miracles. (More on her in just a moment.)

This is a place where our sanctified imaginations can run wild, because Magdala was such an ordinary town, full of ordinary people whom God chose to write into His extraordinary story. You stand here and think, *Anything can happen with God!*

I don't know about you, but I'm ready to discover more about the miracles Jesus did and the lives He radically transformed in this area. If you're ready too, let's visit the very humble but mighty Magdala.

It's time to watch the video for this stop.
Settle in for a few minutes and scan the QR code (access code: Journey).

Drop a Pin

- **Where are you right now in relation to what I spoke about in this section's video? Excited? Curious? Lost? Jot down your thoughts in the space below.**

GOD USES WILLING HEARTS IN REMARKABLE WAYS

Read Your Map

> After this, Jesus traveled about from one town and village to another, proclaiming the good news of the kingdom of God. The Twelve were with him, and also some women who had been cured of evil spirits and diseases: Mary (called Magdalene) from whom seven demons had come out; Joanna the wife of Chuza, the manager of Herod's household; Susanna; and many others. These women were helping to support them out of their own means. (Luke 8:1–3)

Next to the ruins, facing out toward the Sea of Galilee, is the Duc in Altum chapel. This beautiful church is sometimes called "the Boat Chapel" because it has an altar shaped like a small boat that looks like it's floating on the sea. The design was inspired by Luke 5:4, when Jesus said to Simon, James, and John (all would-be disciples), "Launch out into the deep" (NKJV).[3] They obeyed, and guess what? They caught so many fish their nets started to break! This chapel is a beautiful nod to Scripture and Jesus' call to all of us to obey Him and draw in as many people as we can with His love.

The Duc in Altum also has a stunning atrium dedicated to honoring and educating others about the women in the Bible, particularly those who helped spread the gospel (the good news about Jesus). There are eight towering stone pillars, representing Mary Magdalene, Susanna, Joanna, Mary (mother of Jesus), Martha, Salome, and Simon Peter's mother-in-law. If you're counting, that's only seven. Where's the eighth? Maybe *you* are that last pillar, because it represents all women of faith through time.[4] How cool is that?

But let's back up to the woman represented on that first pillar. She is popularly known as Mary Magdalene. But Magdalene wasn't her last name; it was sort of a nickname referencing her hometown. She was born right here, and her name literally means "Mary from Magdala."

While researching Mary Magdalene, I came across this incredible statement about her: "St. Jerome said that Mary was rightly called 'Magdalene,' that is, 'the one of the tower,' because of her singular faith and unwavering courage."[5] What a compliment!

Mary started out from this small fishing town as a woman who was possessed by demons, but her encounter with Jesus transformed her entire life.

- **Take a look at Luke 8:2. What does it say that Jesus healed Mary of?**

By this information alone, Mary Magdalene reveals to us that God loves to do extraordinary things through people and places that are often overlooked.

- **Read John 19:25 and write down who was standing by the cross of Jesus.**

- **Now let's take a look at John 20:11–18. Who stood weeping outside of Jesus' tomb after He was crucified? What happened?**

Group Discussion Prompt

- What "ordinary" places has God used in your life to do something extraordinary or bring transformation?
- How does your place of origin play a role in the way you encountered Jesus and your testimony today?

What I love about Mary is that she didn't ever let her past disqualify her from serving Jesus and others. As a result, she was the very first person to see the resurrected Jesus and be entrusted with the most important message in all of history. She told the disciples, "I have seen the Lord!" (John 20:18). She knew Jesus was alive!

It's pretty easy to disqualify ourselves, isn't it? I don't come from a religious pedigree. I am not the smartest man in the world. I have made loads of mistakes (just ask Sweet Maria). It's tempting for me to think that I shouldn't be the one to share a message or write a Bible study. I'm just a guy who loves balloons and putting a smile on people's faces. By worldly standards, I'm not qualified to do too much. Do you think like this sometimes too?

- **What are you tempted to disqualify yourself from doing right now because of your past?**

- **What are you telling yourself, and how does it compare to what you feel God is telling you?**

Here's the wake-up call God gave me: If I really am so unfit to do stuff, then I probably can't be trusted to decide whether I or anyone else is qualified for anything. The only one who is entirely fit to love others and care for the world with excellence is God. So maybe I should let Him do the qualifying.

The funny thing is, whatever seems disqualifying in your past is what God usually sees as the precise qualification for carrying His message. God isn't looking for people who have it all together. He's looking for people like us, like Mary Magdalene, who know that we're not good enough but that God is more than enough. We're so unqualified that God has had to show up on our behalf and change our lives around. Because we've witnessed the wild transformation of our own lives, we can trust that God can do it again for someone else.

I think it's amazing that Mary of Magdala was chosen to be the first to see the risen Lord. How beautifully it reveals that God uses ordinary people with willing hearts in remarkable ways.

Drop a Pin

- **In the backward way that God does things, what mess-ups or mistakes allowed you to encounter God and qualify you to carry His message?**

THE MAGNIFICENCE OF NOTHING

Read Your Map

> Jesus called his disciples to him and said, "I have compassion for these people; they have already been with me three days and have nothing to eat. I do not want to send them away hungry, or they may collapse on the way."
>
> His disciples answered, "Where could we get enough bread in this remote place to feed such a crowd?"
>
> "How many loaves do you have?" Jesus asked.
>
> "Seven," they replied, "and a few small fish."
>
> He told the crowd to sit down on the ground. Then he took the seven loaves and the fish, and when he had given thanks, he broke them and gave them to the disciples, and they in turn to the people. They all ate and were satisfied. Afterward the disciples picked up seven basketfuls of broken pieces that were left over. The number of those who ate was four thousand men, besides women and children. After Jesus had sent the crowd away, he got into the boat and went to the vicinity of Magadan. (Matt. 15:32–39)

Before arriving at Magdala, Jesus had done some incredible things. He had healed crowds on a mountainside, fed over four thousand people with a little boy's Lunchable, and walked on water (Matt. 14–15). After all these huge moments, Jesus seemed to do something random—He got on a boat and headed toward Magdala. The Bible doesn't mention it here, but we can logically assume the disciples were with Him, because they followed Jesus everywhere He went. They were also present for the next lesson.

Now imagine Jesus and the twelve disciples all piled into a tiny fishing boat to travel a few hours from the eastern side of the Sea of Galilee. The disciples were probably full of energy after watching these incredible miracles. Maybe they asked, "Hey, Jesus, what awesome thing is next? What big city are we heading toward?" And Jesus replied, "Let's go to Magdala."

You would have been able to hear a pin drop (or maybe a fish plop, since I don't think they had pins back then). As the boat rocked up and down on the waves, riding the breeze toward their destination, the disciples were probably pretty quiet. I'm sure some "What is He *thinking*?" looks were passed between them.

To their shock and ours, guess what happened when they arrived. Nothing. The Bible records no miracles, parables, or confrontations of any kind in Magdala. All we know is that Jesus went there. The end. Which leaves us to speculate: Why?

- **Why do you think Jesus headed off to an insignificant, quiet town after being on such an incredible ministry roll? What can you learn from Jesus' decision?**

- **Read the following passages and write down what they all have in common: Matthew 14:13, 23; Mark 1:35; 6:31; Luke 5:15–16; 6:12.**

Many of these verses seem a little boring because they lack action, right? But they serve as evidence that Jesus loved quiet, simple, remote places. Nothing magnificent was set to happen in Magdala. And yet—Jesus came.

Jesus made the nothingness magnificent by His very presence.

Group Discussion Prompt

- In your life, when you feel like nothing significant is happening, do you tend to feel overlooked? Where do you think God is when you're not witnessing breakthroughs or miracles?
- How can you remind yourself that even the quiet place is important to Jesus?

Lack of visible results isn't proof that God isn't acting. Jesus shows up in our lives in every situation. He's there in the busy and the slow. His presence is always with us. We don't magically activate it through crazy schedules. Truthfully, we can get so busy doing "work for God" that we actually become ineffective. Jesus knew this, which is why He set an example for us to consistently withdraw before massive ministry and decision-making moments. We cannot run on empty. We were designed to get quiet to let God's voice fill us.

Take a minute and follow me here: What if Jesus' arrival is the miracle?

You could probably quote this next verse by heart, but we need to bring it up in this space, and I'm asking God to give you a fresh understanding of it.

- **Look up John 3:16 and write down what it says in the space below.**

You see, Jesus is the gift! Not the miracles He did. Not the lessons He taught. Not the laughter He shared across tables at meals. Not the way He loved the little children. Yes, these are all spectacular things that came along with Jesus showing up on this planet. But the real gift is Jesus Himself.

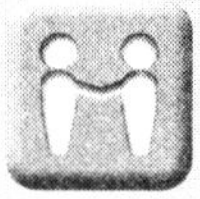

Find Your Friends

Often, the people who are hardest to love need love the most. Sometimes these people are doubting or angry at God because they're experiencing their own "Magdala moment," a time when God seems quiet and nothing seems to be happening.

Over the years, I've discovered that it's not really our job to "fix" anyone's theology. We're just supposed to love no matter what. We're supposed to model for them that faith isn't fragile. God can handle our doubts and questions, so we must accept others in the middle of their wrestling. We've all had moments like this, right? Following God is complex. But we don't need to be afraid of the mystery of how He's working in our lives or the lives of others.

Here's my advice for loving friends who are walking through "Magdala moments." Apply no shame, no defensiveness, and no pressure on them to resolve their conflict with God quickly. Just offer them grace-filled friendship.

- **How do you think we can love our doubting friends in a way that reflects the patience and presence of Jesus?**

- **How can we use Jesus' trip to Magdala as a reminder to them that He is still present even when there isn't a lot of visible action going on?**

- **How can we encourage others that a lack of breakthrough doesn't have to lead to a breakdown of faith?**

Natalie Grant has a beautiful song called "More Than Anything" that we all would be wise to take as a prayer when we visit our own personal Magdala moments. She sings about wanting the Healer more than healing. She encourages us to want Jesus above anything else He could possibly give us.

So, in the time between miracles and mountaintop moments, we must worship Jesus and trust. After all, humble and hidden seasons often prove to be the most important.

Drop a Pin

- **What does it look like for you to trust Jesus and be grateful for the gift of His presence when you experience downtime? How can you follow His lead when He pulls you into a "Magdala moment" to withdraw and rest?**

JESUS CROSSES EVERY BOUNDARY TO REACH US

Read Your Map

> They went across the lake to the region of the Gerasenes. When Jesus got out of the boat, a man with an impure spirit came from the tombs to meet him. This man lived in the tombs, and no one could bind him anymore, not even with a chain. For he had often been chained hand and foot, but he tore the chains apart and broke the irons on his feet. No one was strong enough to subdue him. Night and day among the tombs and in the hills he would cry out and cut himself with stones.
>
> When he saw Jesus from a distance, he ran and fell on his knees in front of him. He shouted at the top of his voice, "What do you want with me, Jesus, Son

> of the Most High God? In God's name don't torture me!" For Jesus had said to him, "Come out of this man, you impure spirit!"
>
> Then Jesus asked him, "What is your name?" ...
>
> A large herd of pigs was feeding on the nearby hillside. The demons begged Jesus, "Send us among the pigs; allow us to go into them." He gave them permission, and the impure spirits came out and went into the pigs. The herd, about two thousand in number, rushed down the steep bank into the lake and were drowned.
>
> Those tending the pigs ran off and reported this in the town and countryside, and the people went out to see what had happened. (Mark 5:1–14)

- **Look back at the beginning of that passage. Where does this Bible passage take place?**

We've learned that Magdala sits on the western shore of the Sea of Galilee, just a hop over from Capernaum. Today, we're going to take a short journey (roughly six miles by boat) across the lake to Gadara. Gadara was part of the Decapolis, which was a group of Gentile cities southeast of the sea.

The Gospels don't give us a ton of information about Gadara itself. What we do know is that Jesus intentionally crossed the lake to reach a demon-possessed man whom most people were afraid of. Honestly, I might have been a little scared too. Think about it: a man with demons who walked among the tombs. It sounds like the setting for a horror movie. Look, I'm a guy who used to hold office hours at Tom Sawyer Island at Disneyland. This is not exactly my cup of tea.

But unlike me, Jesus wasn't scared. He didn't look at this man with fear, nor did He shame him. Instead, He moved toward him. *Jesus was constantly going where others wouldn't.*

A Gentile city like Gadara was considered "unclean" to the Jews. Jewish people were the twelve tribes of Israel, God's chosen people. Gentiles, on the other hand, were outsiders to the covenant God had made with the Jewish people. On top of that, Gadara would have had a

Greek-influenced, or Hellenistic, culture. This means they did not follow the God of the Bible but instead worshipped multiple gods and took part in many pagan practices.

Pig herding was also evidently common in Gadara, something that would have been completely forbidden by Jews. According to the laws of the Torah, the earliest Bible books, a person or place was defiled if pigs were eaten or even touched. All this adds up to making Gadara a place where no Jew would ever want to go.

When Jesus decided to go to Gadara, He wasn't just making a casual trip across the lake. He was intentionally defying geographical, spiritual, and cultural boundaries—all to reach a man who needed Him.

- **Take a moment to reflect: What boundaries did Jesus cross to reach you?**

- **Whom do you think Jesus is calling you to reach, even if doing so would make you uncomfortable? Write down a few names in the space below.**

- **The world had written off this man among the tombs. Look again at Mark 5:3–5. What does it say that no one could do for him? What was he doing to cause himself pain?**

Here is a man who was totally isolated, harming himself, and being spiritually tormented. And everyone had just given up on him. This is terrible!

I met a guy like this once. He was a witch doctor in Uganda who had committed horrible crimes, some that involved hurting children. I visited him a lot in prison, and eventually we became friends. Through our connection, I was able to tell him about Jesus and extend to him God's grace. Amazingly, he came to faith in Jesus. He went from casting curses to telling everyone about hope and redemption. Isn't that incredible?

Read the following verses and write down what stands out to you about how we are to love each other.

- Matthew 22:39

- Luke 6:35

- John 13:34–35

- Romans 13:8–10

As I said in my book *Everybody, Always*, "Jesus didn't say to love people who are easy to love. He said to love everybody. Always."[6]

Here's what loving others and walking with Jesus has taught me: Every person is a story in motion, and God isn't done with any of us or anything yet!

Take a look back at Mark 5:19. After Jesus casts the demons out of this man, what does He command the man to do? Fill in the blank:

Group Discussion Prompt

- Have you ever written anyone off as "too far gone" or seen someone who had been labeled a lost cause?
- Have you ever felt like something in your life was past redemption?

Go home to your own people and tell them ____________________

____

____

____

____

____.

This demon-possessed man found freedom in Jesus and became the first Christian missionary to the Gentiles. Can you believe it? Jesus is amazing, isn't He? He's always setting people free and sending people out to tell others. He's forever been seeking those in darkness, putting light inside of people, and asking them to take that fire and spread it throughout the world.

The truth is that experiencing freedom in Christ always sends us out to tell others. Because of course we want others to have the freedom we have found!

I want to wrap up our time here in Magdala by saying this: This man whom Jesus set free is evidence that when we're faithful to the cause of being a light in a dark world, it can change everything.

What if we decided right here and now to be faithful to being a light?

Sure, there's some crazy stuff going on in life right now. Things aren't always what they should be. But maybe God is at work in a way we can't understand, and maybe we decide to do what this crazy guy did: run with the light inside of us toward the darkness. We can tell everyone what we've seen God do in our own lives and watch the light spread.

When we journey with Jesus into the secret Magdala moments and love the prickly people in uncomfortable Gadara spaces, we may get the opportunity to see people, cities, and entire nations be transformed by God's grace and mercy.

What are you waiting for? Go tell the world about the Light you've found!

Personal Travel Log

Reach deep. In Magdala, we discovered the significance of the secret places. Even when nothing big is happening, Jesus is still showing up in the smallest moments. His presence itself is the treasure, even if we cannot point to any other blessings happening. When we feel lost or lonely, we can rest assured that Jesus is seeking us out and calling us to true freedom. Then we get the wonderful job of extending that freedom to others.

- **What is your key takeaway from this section?**

- **Where do you see God at work in your life and in the lives of others around you?**

- **What is God calling you to do in light of our time in Magdala?**

- **What direction do you think He wants you to go next?**

Pray

Jesus,

You are the God who steps into forgotten places and calls forgotten people by name. You go where no one else will go to love those no one else would love. You did that in the first century, and You still do that today.

Thank You for coming close to me when I was stuck in shame and silence, and thank You for not waiting until I had it all together. You found me, like Mary Magdelene, in the middle of my mess and loved me anyway.

Like Mary, I want to live with courage. I want to love You more than anything. Help me be the kind of disciple who sticks close … even at the cross, even in the silence, even in the garden of grief.

Jesus, when life feels quiet like at Magdala—when there are no fireworks, no breakthroughs, no answers—I don't want to miss You. Teach me to see that Your presence is the miracle.

Help me also to love like You did in Gadara. Give me eyes to see the person the world has written off. Let Your love shine through me to cross boundaries, break rules, and reach into tomb-like places to bring the hope of resurrection. Remind me that no one is beyond Your grace … not even me.

You don't wait for us to come to You; You come to us. You pursue us with purpose. You cast out shame. You replace torment with peace. And then You send us out to tell the story. So today, Jesus, send me. I'll go. I'll carry Your light wherever You lead.

Even in Magdala moments, when nothing big seems to be happening, You're still here. And that's treasure enough.

Amen.

Extend Your Stay

If you want to spend a little more time at this stop, scan the QR code here (access code: Journey). You can tour Magdala, download a digital recipe, and find cool links.

Recipe

Mersu

Don't you think it's time for a dessert? To me, dessert says, "It's time to celebrate!" And it is! Together, we've made it through Capernaum and through the valley of the shadow of death. Now we're in the seaside town of Magdala, and I have found a recipe for an ancient sweet treat made up of staple foods from this region. It's called mersu. Feel free to double or even triple this recipe to share with your Bible study group, neighbors, or friends.

Mersu is simple, using only a few ingredients, like dates, nuts, and honey. It's crazy to think that Jesus and the disciples probably would have eaten mersu, because it was a staple in the diets of ancient Israelites and common to this region of Galilee.[7]

Find a candle and whip out a party hat. Let's try mersu!

YOU WILL NEED:

1 cup pitted dates
½ cup chopped nuts (most recipes use pistachios, but you can choose walnuts or almonds instead)
1 tablespoon honey
Pinch of cinnamon or cardamom (optional)

DIRECTIONS:

1. Soak dates in warm water for about 10 minutes until softened. Then drain and pat dry.
2. Create a date paste by mashing the dates with a fork or a food processor.
3. Add the nuts, honey, and cinnamon or cardamom and mix well.
4. Form paste into small balls or flatten them into disks like a small cookie.
5. Refrigerate for at least 30 minutes or until firm.

Your friends will have as much fun making them with you as eating them with you!*

*Based on a recipe from https://eatshistory.com/mesopotamian-recipe-mersu-dessert-balls.

The Western Wall
(Jerusalem)

STOP 4

BREAKING DOWN DIVIDERS AT THE WESTERN WALL

Bob's Travel Log

Today we're at the Western Wall, the place where the Holy Land all seems to come together. This site is vital to the world's three greatest religions: Judaism, Islam, and Christianity. What that means is that it's a pretty busy place.

People wander through the cobbled Old City streets to flock to this site for personal and spiritual reasons. Many want to see the places where God has touched earth, where much of Jesus' ministry took place, and where the foundations of their faiths were laid. Others want to write out a special prayer and place the scrap into a crack in the Western Wall. Some just want to be in a space that is considered holy in hopes that it may heal their hearts. I think many are here for a bit of all these reasons and more.

Right now, it's early morning. We had to head out at the beginning of the day because we were told that if you want a good view at this site, you need to beat the crowds. After sipping a cup of coffee so strong I was convinced it could have powered our airplane, I found myself overlooking the Dome of the Rock glistening in the sun, taking in the ancient architecture of the Temple Mount, and pondering the prayers of the masses of people gathering at the Western Wall.

From this view, I'm inspired to pray with purpose. Those ancient cracks can hold only small pieces of paper. I actually think that's a good thing. Sometimes the most courageous prayers are the shortest ones. "God, help." "Lead me." "Why?" "Heal her." "Bless him." "Send me." Or just, "Jesus ..."

Gazing at those two-thousand-year-old stones full of rolled-up paper prayers, I'm struck by how desperately humans want to connect with God. I'm so grateful that we can speak with God freely and that His presence is no longer waiting behind any wall. Because of Jesus, experiencing God is no longer limited to temple sites. He's with us on early-morning commutes, in sticky situations, and at kitchen tables and kids' soccer games. Still, there's something sacred about showing up. Physically. Emotionally. Spiritually.

It's humbling to be here at the Temple Mount and Western Wall. These stones are no longer a barrier to keep unholy, messy people like you and me out of a perfect God's presence. They are now a reminder that God meets us wherever we are. That He hears even the smallest of prayers. And that maybe, no matter what religion or walk of life we come from, we're all just hoping to hear the whisper that we're still loved, that God is with us, and that we're never too far gone.

I think I'll carry that whisper home with me.

It's time to watch the video for this stop.
Settle in for a few minutes and scan the QR code (access code: Journey).

Drop a Pin

- **Where are you right now in relation to what I spoke about in this section's video? Excited? Curious? Lost? Jot down your thoughts in the space below.**

ENTERING THE HOLY PLACE AT THE TEMPLE MOUNT

Read Your Map

Then Solomon began to build the temple of the LORD in Jerusalem on Mount Moriah, where the LORD had appeared to his father David. It was on the threshing floor of Araunah the Jebusite, the place provided by David. He began building on the second day of the second month in the fourth year of his reign.

The foundation Solomon laid for building the temple of God was sixty cubits long and twenty cubits wide (using the cubit of the old standard). The portico at the front of the temple was twenty cubits long across the width of the building and twenty cubits high.

He overlaid the inside with pure gold. He paneled the main hall with juniper and covered it with fine gold and decorated it with palm tree and chain designs. He adorned the temple with precious stones. And the gold he used was gold of Parvaim. He overlaid the ceiling beams, doorframes, walls and doors of the temple with gold, and he carved cherubim on the walls.

He built the Most Holy Place, its length corresponding to the width of the temple—twenty cubits long and twenty cubits wide. He overlaid the inside with six hundred talents of fine gold. The gold nails weighed fifty shekels. He also overlaid the upper parts with gold.

> For the Most Holy Place he made a pair of sculptured cherubim and overlaid them with gold. The total wingspan of the cherubim was twenty cubits. One wing of the first cherub was five cubits long and touched the temple wall, while its other wing, also five cubits long, touched the wing of the other cherub. Similarly one wing of the second cherub was five cubits long and touched the other temple wall, and its other wing, also five cubits long, touched the wing of the first cherub. The wings of these cherubim extended twenty cubits. They stood on their feet, facing the main hall.
>
> He made the curtain of blue, purple and crimson yarn and fine linen, with cherubim worked into it.
>
> For the front of the temple he made two pillars, which together were thirty-five cubits long, each with a capital five cubits high. He made interwoven chains and put them on top of the pillars. He also made a hundred pomegranates and attached them to the chains. He erected the pillars in the front of the temple, one to the south and one to the north. The one to the south he named Jakin and the one to the north Boaz. (2 Chron. 3:1–17)

If you've ever read the Bible and thought, *Did this stuff really happen?* then standing here at the Temple Mount might make you lean more toward believing. You might even come to wonder if perhaps everything in the Bible might actually *be* true. This is the place where the first, second, and third Jewish temples (Solomon's, Zerubbabel's, and Herod's) were built. It's also believed to be Mount Moriah, the spot where Abraham was sent to sacrifice Isaac. It's certainly the location of Herod's Temple, which Jesus visited throughout His life. Being surrounded by so much historical evidence of God's actions here on earth is wild, mysterious, and exciting.

The specifics we just read about for the First Temple can seem like nothing more than a bunch of information and measurements. But what they truly offer us is an inside look at what it might have been like to walk into Solomon's ancient temple. It brings to life the ways people used to connect with God.

When Solomon completed the temple, it was a gigantic masterpiece of a building crafted by the best artists and dedicated to the glory of God. There was an outer courtyard, the Court of the Gentiles, where non-Jews would gather (you and I might have hung out there). Then there was the Court of the Women, where Jewish women could come. Moving inward from there was the Court of the Israelites, where Jewish men could come.

Inside the building itself was the Holy Place, which contained a golden lampstand, the table of showbread (a sacrificial offering of bread), and an incense altar. The priests could enter here. The most sacred place of all was the Most Holy Place. This was an inner room hidden behind a giant curtain. It was where God's presence would dwell on earth before Jesus existed. Only the high priest could enter the Most Holy Place, and he could do that only once a year.

- **Read Hebrews 9:3–7. According to God's instructions, what did the high priest have to do before he entered the Most Holy Place?**

- **Now read Leviticus 16:2. When God first established the Most Holy Place, Aaron was declared the first Levitical high priest. What were the consequences he would face if he did not enter properly?**

Yowza! This is serious, right? God's presence is so holy and powerful that it would take out somebody who wasn't a Levitical priest and hadn't purified himself. You know what this means? It means that you and I would have been left in that outer courtyard longing to know what it felt like to be close to God and never knowing. But check this out ...

Read Matthew 27:51 and fill in the blanks:

> At that moment the curtain of the temple was torn in two from ____________
> to ____________________________.

This is incredible news! There used to be boundaries between all of us and God. We had to go through the right person, say the right words, follow all the right rules just to get close to our

Group Discussion Prompt

Sometimes I get so busy chasing every crazy idea that I forget what a gift it is to have free access to the God of the universe. If I'm honest, my busyness and distractions are a barrier that tends to come between God and me. Instead of letting these walls stand, Jesus in me gives me the ability to knock them down, clear the clutter (and my schedule), and just be with God. What about you?

- Why do you think God originally created boundaries in the temple? What do you think those boundaries taught people about Him?
- What does it mean that the curtain was torn from top to bottom? Why do you think that detail matters?
- Why do we sometimes still live like the veil hasn't been torn?
- What might it look like for our group to be a "no-curtain community"–a place where people feel free to come to God together, just as they are?

Creator. And that was only if we were Jewish, male, and a priest of the tribe of Levi.

But Jesus came and *ripped the veil from top to bottom*—literally. Now? Now, the door's wide open to encounter God's presence. No password, no secret knock. We don't have to be perfect, polished, or put together.

We just have to come.

God's love for us is so awesome that it kicks down the barriers and says, "Let's be together." We used to stand on the outside hoping. Now we walk right into God's presence—like kids running into their Father's arms.

Drop a Pin

Pretend we jumped back in time and we're standing at the temple. The veil has been torn, and we're able, for the first time ever, to walk into the throne room of God. There's no curtain and no security check ... it's just wide open. God looks at you and smiles.

- **What do you say to Him?**

- **What do you think He might say back?**

LAYING A FAITH FOUNDATION AT THE DOME OF THE ROCK

Read Your Map

Some time later God tested Abraham. He said to him, "Abraham!"

"Here I am," he replied.

Then God said, "Take your son, your only son, whom you love—Isaac—and go to the region of Moriah. Sacrifice him there as a burnt offering on a mountain I will show you."

Early the next morning Abraham got up and loaded his donkey. He took with him two of his servants and his son Isaac. When he had cut enough wood for the burnt offering, he set out for the place God had told him about. On the third day Abraham looked up and saw the place in the distance. He said to his servants, "Stay here with the donkey while I and the boy go over there. We will worship and then we will come back to you."

Abraham took the wood for the burnt offering and placed it on his son Isaac, and he himself carried the fire and the knife. As the two of them went on together, Isaac spoke up and said to his father Abraham, "Father?"

"Yes, my son?" Abraham replied.

"The fire and wood are here," Isaac said, "but where is the lamb for the burnt offering?"

Abraham answered, "God himself will provide the lamb for the burnt offering, my son." And the two of them went on together.

When they reached the place God had told him about, Abraham built an altar there and arranged the wood on it. He bound his son Isaac and laid him on the altar, on top of the wood. Then he reached out his hand and took the knife to slay his son. But the angel of the LORD called out to him from heaven, "Abraham! Abraham!"

"Here I am," he replied.

> "Do not lay a hand on the boy," he said. "Do not do anything to him. Now I know that you fear God, because you have not withheld from me your son, your only son."
>
> Abraham looked up and there in a thicket he saw a ram caught by its horns. He went over and took the ram and sacrificed it as a burnt offering instead of his son. So Abraham called that place The LORD Will Provide. And to this day it is said, "On the mountain of the LORD it will be provided."
>
> The angel of the LORD called to Abraham from heaven a second time and said, "I swear by myself, declares the LORD, that because you have done this and have not withheld your son, your only son, I will surely bless you and make your descendants as numerous as the stars in the sky and as the sand on the seashore. Your descendants will take possession of the cities of their enemies, and through your offspring all nations on earth will be blessed, because you have obeyed me." (Gen. 22:1–18)

The Dome of the Rock was built in the late seventh century (around AD 691) by the Umayyads, an ancient Islamic dynasty. Muslims revere the location for different reasons than Jews and Christians do. Jews and Christians identify it as Mount Moriah, the place where Abraham prepared to sacrifice Isaac.

It's a hard scene to picture—Abraham walking with his son toward this rock, thinking God might actually call him to sacrifice his beloved child.

- **Let's pause right here and think a little about the Old and New Testament. How do you think Abraham's willingness to offer Isaac foreshadows God's offering of Jesus?**

Find Your Friends

We're not naturally sacrificial people, are we? We spend so much time trying to protect our time, our money, and our platforms. But Abraham was willing to let that all go for God. And consider Jesus: He didn't protect anything. He poured it all out. Not for applause but for love.

So maybe being a sacrificial person isn't about dramatic gestures. Maybe it's about daily surrenders. Leaving a little room in your calendar to be interruptible. Leaving the last word unsaid to allow reconciliation. Leaving a parking spot closer to the restaurant for someone else and walking farther because you're able.

- **Do you know someone who loves others sacrificially? What do they do?**

- **What can you do today to thank them and to love someone courageously too?**

The chart on the next page shows a list of verses (on the left) and a list of statements about Abraham and Isaac foreshadowing Jesus' sacrifice and resurrection (on the right). Draw a line between the verse and its matching statement. (Answers on page 173.)

Verses	Foreshadowing
For God so loved the world that he gave his one and only Son, that whoever believes in him shall not perish but have eternal life. (John 3:16)	Mount Moriah, where Abraham offered Isaac, later became the site of the Temple Mount—the very place where Jesus would later be condemned and sacrificed nearby (Golgotha is within walking distance).
He who did not spare his own Son, but gave him up for us all—how will he not also, along with him, graciously give us all things? (Rom. 8:32)	In writing this verse, Paul used similar language as Genesis 22:12—"You have not withheld from me your son"—to describe God's gift.
Behold! The Lamb of God who takes away the sin of the world! (John 1:29 NKJV)	Though written centuries after Abraham, Isaiah's suffering servant fulfills the picture Abraham had anticipated: a Son who would willingly carry the wood (cross), be bound, and be offered.
By faith Abraham, when God tested him, offered Isaac as a sacrifice.... Abraham reasoned that God could even raise the dead. (Heb. 11:17-19)	This verse reflects on Abraham's faith, seeing it as a herald to resurrection hope—fulfilled in Christ.
Then Solomon began to build the temple of the LORD in Jerusalem on Mount Moriah, where the LORD had appeared to his father David. (2 Chron. 3:1)	Isaac is Abraham's "only son," offered in radical obedience and love—mirroring Jesus as God's only Son. God's act of giving His Son echoes Abraham's willingness to give Isaac. God did not hold back.
The LORD has laid on Him the iniquity of us all.... He was led like a lamb to the slaughter. (Isa. 53:6-7)	Jesus is the Lamb that Abraham believed God would provide, finally revealed.

The ruins at the Temple Mount are tangible reminders that the foundation of our faith was laid at the cost of obedience, tremendous sacrifice, and the depth of God's provision.

Like the ram in the thicket, Jesus was provided on our behalf and sacrificed in our place ... not on the rock but on the cross.

Group Discussion Prompt

- In what ways do physical places help us reflect on spiritual truths? Is there a spot that makes you think more about God? Where is it? Tell us about it!

Drop a Pin

- **If you were standing at the Dome of the Rock today, knowing what happened on that mountain, what would you say to God?**

- **How does understanding this location deepen your gratitude for Christ's sacrifice?**

CONNECTING WITH GOD AT THE WESTERN WALL

Read Your Map

But will God really dwell on earth? The heavens, even the highest heaven, cannot contain you. How much less this temple I have built! Yet give attention to your servant's prayer and his plea for mercy, LORD my God. Hear the cry and the prayer that your servant is praying in your presence this day. May your eyes be open toward this temple night and day, this place of which you said, "My

> Name shall be there," so that you will hear the prayer your servant prays toward this place. Hear the supplication of your servant and of your people Israel when they pray toward this place. Hear from heaven, your dwelling place, and when you hear, forgive. (1 Kings 8:27–30)

The Western Wall is a remnant of the massive retaining wall that once supported the Second Temple, destroyed in AD 70 by the Romans. For non-Muslims, it is the closest you can get to where the Most Holy Place once stood. It's sometimes referred to as "the Wailing Wall" because for centuries people from all walks of life traveled here to pray, weep, and tuck notes to God into its ancient crevices.

It's amazing to stand at this wall and see droves of individuals seeking God. It truly feels like a "thin place," where heaven touches earth.

- **Read Luke 2:46–49. What was Jesus found doing in the temple as a boy?**

- **Look at Matthew 24:1–2. What did Jesus say would happen to this temple?**

- **What does 1 Corinthians 3:16 point to as the temple of God now?**

We are now the temple of God. How amazing is that! This doesn't mean we have it all together. It means that God wanted to be close. So close that He moved in.

If you've ever thought God was far away, you were looking in the wrong direction. He's not across town or in a distant sanctuary. We don't have to make the trek to the Western Wall. He's in us, with us, all around us—cheering us on like a proud dad at his third-grade kid's soccer game.

Sticking a piece of paper into the Western Wall is a great way to pray specifically. God knows everything, so it's not like He needs us to tell Him our requests. I think one of the purposes of prayer is for us to make our requests known to ourselves so that we can make them known to God. The more specific we are, the better we can see God's answer. Does that make sense?

Group Discussion Prompt

- If you really believed you were God's temple, how would it change the way you saw yourself today?
- What keeps you from talking to God freely—and what do you think He would say about that?

When we're vague with God, praying something like, "God, I'm so stressed out right now," we're not asking for anything in particular. How will we know if God answers that prayer? But when we come to Him and say, "Here are the four things that are freaking me out," then if He grants that request, we will definitely see it. Then we can understand what God did. So let us come to God and say, "Would you please help me with these exact things?"

I know, I come across as a very bluntly outgoing guy. You're thinking, *Must be easy for you to say, Bob*. But the truth is that I'm tremendously insecure. Go ask any of my friends or Sweet Maria. For me, what praying specifically looks like is this: Instead of saying, "Hey, God, help me with all my insecurities," I would pray, "What is it that that's connected to my insecurity? Is it linked to a feeling that if somebody actually got to know me, they would not want to have anything to do with me? Is that crazy? Please show me the root of this and help me pull it out." When we pray like this and God answers, we notice.

Personal Travel Log

Reach deep. At the Western Wall, we discovered the power of God's presence and the importance of praying specifically. We can love others freely and sacrificially because of what Jesus did for us on the cross, tearing the veil so He could meet with us and live in our hearts.

- **What is your key takeaway from this section?**

- **Where do you see God at work in your life and in the lives of others around you?**

- **What is God calling you to do in light of our time at the Western Wall?**

- **What direction do you think He wants you to go next?**

Pray

God,

Thanks for being the kind of God who doesn't wait behind a curtain anymore. You ripped that thing top to bottom just to make it clear that we don't need the right words or the right clothes or the right background. We just need to show up.

And so here we are—showing up. A little distracted, a little messy, but fully Yours.

Being here at the Western Wall, or even just thinking about it, reminds us that You've always been a God who wants to be close. People still write prayers and tuck them into stone. But now that You're risen from the dead, You write Your name on our hearts and tuck Your Spirit inside us. That's incredible.

Thank You for reminding us that we're the temple now. Not because we've got it all figured out, but because You moved in. And You're not moving out.

Help us be the kind of people who make space: for You, for others, for grace to do what it does best. Help us give up the front-row parking spot, the last word, the perfectly planned schedule. Let us live like love matters most, because it does.

And if there's anyone still standing at a distance thinking they don't belong with You, use us to throw the doors wide open. We want our lives to shout what You've been whispering all along: *You are not too far gone. I'm still here. And I love you like crazy.*

Thanks for being better than we imagined and closer than we deserve.

In Jesus' name, amen.

Extend Your Stay

If you want to spend a little more time at this stop, scan the QR code here (access code: Journey). You can tour the Western Wall, download a digital recipe, and find cool links.

Recipe

Jerusalem-Style Mixed Grill

(ME'ORAV YERUSHALMI)

If we were to head toward the Western Wall in Jerusalem, we'd pass a vibrant, thriving street-food scene in the Jewish Quarter, just outside the Old City gates. The smells there are incredible. Traditional foods like falafel (crispy chickpea balls in pita with salad and tahini) and bourekas (flaky pastries filled with cheese, potato, or mushroom) are freshly made and sold in the Old City, while fresh juice is pressed and nuts are roasted on the more modern outdoor shopping street of the Mamilla Mall. Bold spices and organic aromas float through the air. It's enough to make all of us hungry and curious about what to try next.

Just a short taxi ride away is Jerusalem's renowned food market, the Mahane Yehuda Market. The market is known for its incredible offerings, especially the Jerusalem mixed grill we're going to try today. This dish is more than just an excellent street food. Jerusalem mixed grill tells the story of the cultural fusion of Jerusalem, a city that is sacred to Christians, Jews, and Muslims alike. You'll find ingredients in this dish that pull from surrounding ethnic roots and meet the dietary guidelines of religions that have dominated this area for centuries.

Mostly what I like about this dish is that it's a fusion of cultures and religions meant to bring us all together.

So grab your friends or Bible study group, gather around the table, and let's try something new together.

YOU WILL NEED:

1 pound chicken thighs or breast, cut into small pieces

½ pound chicken hearts and/or liver (optional)

1 large onion, sliced

3 tablespoons olive oil
Juice of half a lemon
1 teaspoon ground cumin
1 teaspoon ground coriander
1 teaspoon paprika
½ teaspoon turmeric
¼ teaspoon cinnamon
Pinch of cayenne or chili flakes for heat (optional)
Pita bread, for serving (optional)
Hummus or Israeli salad, for serving (optional)
Pickles, for serving (optional)

DIRECTIONS:

1. Combine the chicken, liver/hearts (if using), onion, olive oil, lemon juice, and all spices. Let sit for 30 minutes (or longer in the fridge) to marinate.
2. Then heat a large skillet or griddle over medium-high heat. Add the entire mixture and sauté for about 10–15 minutes until the meat is browned and fully cooked and the onions are soft and caramelized.
3. Spoon into pita bread with hummus, Israeli salad (diced cucumber, tomato, parsley, lemon, and olive oil), and/or pickles for a true street-food experience.

You and your friends might consider eating these outdoors for a more authentic street-food atmosphere.*

*Based on a recipe from www.israelcart.com/recipes/jerusalem-mixed-grill.

Caesarea by the Sea

STOP 5

SHARING A MESSAGE AT CAESAREA BY THE SEA

Bob's Travel Log

Today I'm standing in a place where ruins whisper and the sea won't stop talking: Caesarea by the Sea. This was the playground of Herod, the king of Judea at the time of Jesus' birth. Later, Paul was thrown into prison here. Caesarea by the Sea was a city built to impress—but now it is mostly held together by memory, salt air, and divine fingerprints.

You can still see the foundation stones of Herod's palace from here, right where the waves crash into what used to be the symbol of human greatness. Herod built colossal structures, possibly hoping he'd be remembered throughout all time. The funny thing is that most people don't remember him for his big buildings; they remember him because he tried to destroy Christianity before it even started.

Herod felt so threatened by the Messiah's arrival that he ordered all Jewish baby boys in Bethlehem to be killed. Warned by an angelic vision, Joseph and Mary rescued the infant Jesus from the massacre, proving that not even political power, fear, or violence can keep God's love from showing up.

The wildest thought I have standing here is that *this* is the place where Paul was held in prison and tried according to Roman law. He sat in chains here. And it was here that he asked to stand before Caesar in Rome. Paul's journey from Caesarea to Rome is how the gospel caught wind and sailed west. Possibly, we all know who Jesus is because Paul decided to launch from this location with the good news. And I think that's where life change begins—not in comfort but in calling. Not with applause, but with obedience.

So I'm standing at the edge of history today, and all I can think is:

Let's launch from here to go love people like we mean it.

It's time to watch the video for this stop.
Settle in for a few minutes and scan the QR code (access code: Journey).

Drop a Pin

- **Where are you right now in relation to what I spoke about in this section's video? Excited? Curious? Lost? Jot down your thoughts in the space below.**

DISCOVERING YOUR LAUNCHING POINT AT CAESAREA BY THE SEA

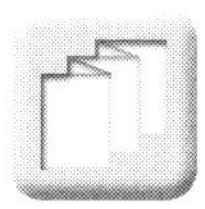

Read Your Map

> After spending eight or ten days with them, Festus went down to Caesarea. The next day he convened the court and ordered that Paul be brought before him. When Paul came in, the Jews who had come down from Jerusalem stood around him. They brought many serious charges against him, but they could not prove them.
>
> Then Paul made his defense: "I have done nothing wrong against the Jewish law or against the temple or against Caesar."
>
> Festus, wishing to do the Jews a favor, said to Paul, "Are you willing to go up to Jerusalem and stand trial before me there on these charges?"
>
> Paul answered: "I am now standing before Caesar's court, where I ought to be tried. I have not done any wrong to the Jews, as you yourself know very well. If, however, I am guilty of doing anything deserving death, I do not refuse to die. But if the charges brought against me by these Jews are not true, no one has the right to hand me over to them. I appeal to Caesar!"
>
> After Festus had conferred with his council, he declared: "You have appealed to Caesar. To Caesar you will go!" (Acts 25:6–12)

Though Jesus isn't recorded as visiting Caesarea, the city was the launching point for a global movement, with people starting to follow the way of Jesus through Paul's mission.

Before we get into all that, let's answer this question: Who was Paul?

Oh man, Paul was a guy who got everything wrong ... until he got it so wonderfully right. He started off hunting Christians—literally dragging them out of their homes (Acts 8:1–3). If you asked the early church who their biggest threat was, they probably wouldn't have said a Roman emperor. They would've pointed to this Jewish Pharisee named Saul of Tarsus.

And yet, he's the guy Jesus picked. Not after he cleaned up his act. Not after a few years of therapy. But right in the middle of his mess. Jesus knocked him off his horse, gave him a new name, and asked him to go change the world. We know him now as the apostle Paul.

- **Read Paul's conversion story in Acts 9:1–22. In your own words, summarize what happened in the space below:**

After his conversion, Paul was shipwrecked, beaten, imprisoned, snakebitten (2 Cor. 11:16–29), and more but still wouldn't stop talking about God's love. He had a message that burned in his bones. Not a rehearsed sermon but a real story about a God who finds people in prisons, storms, and deserts and says, "I choose you."

Paul didn't wait until he was understood to start loving people. He didn't wait to have the right title or the right words. He just kept going. And he wrote half the New Testament along the way. Not bad for a guy nobody trusted at first.

The Bible zeroes in on three main missionary journeys for Paul. The first is in Acts 13–14, a journey that took him throughout Asia Minor with a friend named Barnabas. We find his second missionary journey in Acts 15–18, where Paul and another friend, Silas, traveled back through Asia Minor and on into Europe, establishing churches. On his final trip, covered in Acts 18–21, Paul spent a lot of his time in Ephesus, Macedonia, Greece, and the surrounding areas before he returned to Jerusalem. For deeper study, go back and read about Paul's missionary journeys in these chapters.

We're going to drop into Paul's story as he wrapped up this third missionary journey.

- **Look up Acts 23:21–35. Why was Paul arrested in Jerusalem? Where did the Romans transfer him?**

Now we're getting somewhere. Paul ends up essentially under house arrest in Caesarea by the Sea.

- **Look up Acts 19:21. Where did Paul declare he must visit?**

Now find Acts 23:11 and fill in the blanks for what the Lord said to Paul:

> The following night the Lord stood near Paul and said, "Take courage! As you have testified about me in ____________________, so you must also testify in ________________."

- **In Acts 27:24, what does the angel say to Paul on a ship in a storm?**

At this point in Paul's life, all signs seemed to be pointing the apostle toward Rome. God used Caesarea by the Sea as the launching point to get him there.

Launching carries a lot of uncertainty, just like a rocket ship at takeoff. Have you ever seen a rocket launch? I haven't in person, but I've watched them on TV. It seems amazing. All that fire, all that noise, all that shaking—and then, "Three, two, one ... liftoff!"

Can you imagine being an astronaut? You're strapped in a projectile headed toward space. You've trained and planned, but there's no way to know for certain what's going to happen. You're just trusting

Group Discussion Prompt

- What places in your life have felt like "launching points"?
- Where has God used something that felt limiting (like prison, for Paul) to expand your faith or influence?

the preparation of your team, the engineers who built your ship, and the instructions from the capsule communicator (capcom).

Capcom is a trained astronaut serving as the single point of communication between mission control and the astronauts in the spacecraft. They offer information, give final instructions, and reassure the crew with countdowns and updates. Capcom is like your most trusted friend in a headset, the one who's walked where you're about to walk. When everything's shaking, they don't give you panic; they give you purpose. They remind you: You're ready!

God is doing the same thing for us today. As we stand on our own launchpads in life, He reassures us that we're ready to trust Him. Telling the world about love and full life isn't rocket science—but it does mean launching into our communities from a place of trust, taking risks, and trusting God for the trajectory.

Drop a Pin

- **As you've stood at launching points in your life, what have you feared the most? Are you standing there right now? Can you identify one area in your life (work, family, church, school) where God may be calling you to live out love more boldly?**

SOMETIMES THE BEST WAY IS TO SHOW, NOT SHOUT

Read Your Map

> About noon the following day as they were on their journey and approaching the city, Peter went up on the roof to pray. He became hungry and wanted something to eat, and while the meal was being prepared, he fell into a trance. He saw heaven opened and something like a large sheet being let down to earth

> by its four corners. It contained all kinds of four-footed animals, as well as reptiles and birds. Then a voice told him, "Get up, Peter. Kill and eat."
>
> "Surely not, Lord!" Peter replied. "I have never eaten anything impure or unclean."
>
> The voice spoke to him a second time, "Do not call anything impure that God has made clean."
>
> This happened three times, and immediately the sheet was taken back to heaven. (Acts 10:9–16)

We're picking up from Paul's mission and jumping over into Peter's vision. And we're going to do that by hopping in the car for a pleasant hour-long drive down the Mediterranean coast from Caesarea to a neighboring area called Joppa. To get there back in biblical times, we would have walked for a few days down the Via Maris (Way of the Sea), which was a major trade road that ran along the coastline. I love a good long walk down the beach as much as anyone, but I say we stick to a modern car and cruise on down to meet up with Peter.

Now, I know that this Bible passage seems like it's about food. However, it is referring to so much more.

Remember how we talked about pigs being unclean for Jewish people? In the Old Testament—called the Tanakh in biblical times and consisting of the Law (Torah, the first five books of the Old Testament), the Prophets (Nevi'im), and the Writings (Ketuvim)—there was a whole list of dietary laws that God's people had to follow to separate Israel from other nations so they could represent God's holiness.

Look up the dietary command given in Leviticus 11:3 and fill in the blanks:

> You may eat any animal that has a ______________________ hoof and that chews the ___________.

- **What reason does God offer for these restrictions** (see v. 44)?

If you keep reading in Leviticus 11 (I encourage you to check out the whole chapter), you'll find a list of clean and unclean animals. I'll summarize it for you like this:

Clean Animal Examples

- Cattle, sheep, goats—vv. 2–3
- Fish with fins and scales—v. 9
- Certain birds like doves

Unclean Animal Examples

- Camel, rabbit, rock hyrax—vv. 4–6
- Pig (does not chew the cud and has a divided hoof)—v. 7
- All shellfish and sea creatures without fins/scales—v. 10
- Predatory birds and scavengers—vv. 13–19
- Most insects (except some locusts)—vv. 20–23

And I thought following keto or the Whole30 diet would be hard. The Israelites had to follow these rules their entire lives.

You know who didn't have to? The Gentiles. Remember them? They were all people groups apart from the Israelites and were outside the covenant of God. They were the ones who, in Gadara, had a whole flock of pigs.

With Peter's vision, God was saying, "The good news of Jesus is now for everybody!" Jesus' death and resurrection was an open invitation for Jews and Gentiles alike to come to the table, because the emphasis was no longer on the rules of religion but on a relationship with God.

This would have probably been really hard for the Jewish Christians to accept. They had grown up drawing a "faith circle" around themselves as God's chosen people. You could tell who was in and who was out by whether they followed the rules of the Torah, including the dietary laws. Now, God was announcing there were no more boundaries. That meant that, because of freedom in Jesus, the circle was enlarged wide enough for everyone on earth to fit in it.

- **Read Mark 7:14–23. How does this statement from Jesus compare to the Jewish laws in Leviticus? What does He say truly makes a person unclean?**

Check out 1 Samuel 16:7 and fill in the blanks:

People look at the ____,
but the LORD looks at the ____________________.

The big shift that happened here at Caesarea by the Sea through Peter's vision is that God called His people away from performance and into His grace. God cares way more about our hearts than our ability to check off everything on a religious list. Sat in church? Check. Didn't lie or steal or cheat? Check. Volunteered somewhere? Check. We can do all these "right" things and still get our relationship with God wrong.

- **Read 1 Corinthians 13:1–3 and summarize in your own words what it says:**

The missing component in the rules of religion is love for God! He wants our hearts. God wishes for us to obey His commands out of an overflow of love of Him. But we can't step inside the soul of someone else to know whether they really love God. So we tend to judge someone by their actions. We push prickly people away or write them out of faith circles because they don't do all the "Christian things" we think they should.

For some inspiration on how to love others well, let's look at a conversation that our main guy for this section, Peter, had with Jesus.

- **Read Matthew 16:15–17, 20. Who does Peter say Jesus is?**

- **After Peter's proclamation, what did Jesus order the disciples to do?**

Find Your Friends

"Don't tell anyone" seems like a crazy thing for Jesus to tell the disciples. I mean, the Messiah was here! This was great news. Shouldn't He have said, "Go shout to the whole world that Love has arrived"? But maybe Jesus really wanted Peter and the disciples to first understand that the best way to spread the message is by showing, not shouting. He didn't want a PR release about His arrival; Jesus wanted changed hearts.

- **Who are the people you tend to avoid that Jesus would likely engage?**

- **Who is one person who makes you uncomfortable who you could show love to with no strings attached (not as a project, just as a person)? What could you do?**

Sometimes we rush to post or preach when instead Jesus is asking us to love someone really well—so they'll see Him without needing a sermon. Don't get me wrong: A good sermon is amazing. But a lot of people out there are scrolling through social media looking for cultural fads rather than Bible-based messages. They'll hang out with some friends over a good cup of coffee but aren't ready to walk into a church. So we get to use our hearts to bring Love to them. We get to show them that the faith circle is so wide that the whole earth, even they, can fit inside and that Jesus has invited everyone in.

Drop a Pin

- **In light of Peter's vision and the challenge to show God's love before we shout it, what do you feel like God is calling you to do?**

- **How has our time in Caesarea by the Sea shaped you so far?**

FINDING YOUR FAST HORSE

Read Your Map

"So then, King Agrippa, I was not disobedient to the vision from heaven. First to those in Damascus, then to those in Jerusalem and in all Judea, and then to the Gentiles, I preached that they should repent and turn to God and demonstrate their repentance by their deeds. That is why some Jews seized me in the temple courts and tried to kill me. But God has helped me to this very day; so I stand here and testify to small and great alike. I am saying nothing beyond what the prophets and Moses

> said would happen—that the Messiah would suffer and, as the first to rise from the dead, would bring the message of light to his own people and to the Gentiles."
>
> At this point Festus interrupted Paul's defense. "You are out of your mind, Paul!" he shouted. "Your great learning is driving you insane."
>
> "I am not insane, most excellent Festus," Paul replied. "What I am saying is true and reasonable. The king is familiar with these things, and I can speak freely to him. I am convinced that none of this has escaped his notice, because it was not done in a corner. King Agrippa, do you believe the prophets? I know you do."
>
> Then Agrippa said to Paul, "Do you think that in such a short time you can persuade me to be a Christian?"
>
> Paul replied, "Short time or long—I pray to God that not only you but all who are listening to me today may become what I am, except for these chains." (Acts 26:19–29)

In our video at Caesarea by the Sea, you heard me refer to Paul Revere. Paul was an early industrialist famous for his "midnight ride," where he warned American colonists that British soldiers were on their way during the Revolutionary War. He was a man with a message. And when Paul Revere needed a fast horse to deliver it, he borrowed one from a friend.

Today, I want to be the friend who helps you discover your own fast horse—a story, tool, or habit that helps you bring the message about Love and Life to other people. Let's do that by taking another look at Paul (the apostle we previously learned about in this section) and his proclamation to Festus and Agrippa while he was held captive here in Caesarea.

In Acts 26, we see that Paul's fast horse was his testimony. Most of this chapter is dedicated to Paul sharing with Festus and Agrippa the story about how he encountered Jesus and how it changed his life. It would be pretty wild to hear Paul say, "Hey, I used to kill Christians, but now I am one." I imagine that had a great impact on Festus. It's a good reminder that our stories carry power.

Read Revelation 12:11 and fill in the blank:

> They triumphed over [Satan] by the blood of the Lamb and by the word of their ______________________________; they did not love their lives so much as to shrink from death.

Our testimony—all that Jesus has done in our lives—and Jesus' sacrifice have the power to actually defeat Satan. Isn't that incredible?

This means that our story is our fast horse. It's how we carry the message of the way God changed our lives into the world around us. Sometimes we tell that story through words, and other times we show our hearts are transformed by something we do.

While you may not consider yourself a "talker," being able to communicate your story is a powerful tool. So, looking at Paul's message, here's a little template to follow to share your own life-changing moments with others:

Start with a story. Paul never offered Festus and Agrippa a sermon. He just shared lived moments that pointed to hope in Jesus and the grace that he was shown.

Choose vulnerability. In Acts 26, Paul was very honest about his mistakes and revealed the unexpected places God showed up. With Agrippa, he knew that honesty would invite connection.

Show love in the telling. Paul made a point to connect with Agrippa on a personal level. He was respectful and showed Agrippa (and Festus) honor. The old saying "No one cares how much you know before they know how much you care" is very true.

Leave space. Don't wrap it up neatly. The end of Paul's declaration was probably challenging for Agrippa to consider. Paul didn't tie everything up in a neat bow. He left Agrippa questioning how Paul could feel freedom in Jesus even as he was bound by chains.

The good news is, our fast horse can be our God-story, but it can also be the way we love others.

Group Discussion Prompt

I've written several books, and I find this formula to be particularly helpful. Because sometimes you just don't know where to start. Sometimes I also don't know how to wrap things up, because I feel like the process of loving people extravagantly is an ongoing discussion. So you know what I do? I put my personal phone number in the back of all my books. If I'm available when people call, I answer. Communication is so powerful, and when we share what God has done in our lives, it reminds people that He can do wild, whimsical, and wonderful things.

Take some time to fill in some of these categories about the story God has given you. Flip to your Personal Travel Log at the end of this section and write your thoughts down. And when you're done, share with your group.

- If you could summarize your message in a few sentences, what would it be? Beyond the words—what's your life saying?

- **According to Matthew 5:16, what should our actions cause other people to do?**

Once, I had been scheduled to speak at an event, and two days before, the pastor called and told me some devastating news: His son had just been diagnosed with leukemia. When I came to speak, I knew the best way for us to love this pastor well was to lift him up. So, instead of having him come down front for everyone to pray for his family, I asked the attendees if they would crowd-surf the pastor. We *literally* held him up that night, and it brought a smile to his face in a dark situation. Thinking out of the box to bring love to this pastor was my fast horse. What's yours?

Some people are great guacamole makers and can bring that over to a friend's house to share. Others own nonprofits or are highly involved in their community. There are people who are super thoughtful and will grab a few extra groceries for a neighbor in need. God has uniquely gifted everyone with a tool or talent to love others well. Lean into it. Hop on your fast horse and rush out with love into the world around you.

Personal Travel Log

Reach deep. At Caesarea by the Sea, we learned that God launches beautiful things from unlikely places. We don't need a stage or a title. Just love. Real, no-agenda, Jesus-kind-of love.

From Paul we learned that big moments with God often begin with surrender. He didn't wait until he wasn't in chains to start moving. Even while arrested and on trial, he brought the gospel into the Western world.

Then there's Peter. A man whose vision taught us that Jesus has a circle that is big enough for everyone. All the rules and religious to-dos might help us live "right," but they don't magically earn us a right relationship with God. So it doesn't matter who we are or what we've done; we can all walk into the wide-open arms of Jesus.

We all have a fast horse—a reason to get moving. That reason is a launchpad for us to get out into our communities and share the love of Jesus. We are leaving Caesarea ready to tell our stories and love people like we mean it.

As you reflect on all you've just learned, consider these questions:

- **What is your key takeaway from this section?**

- **Where do you see God at work in your life and in the lives of others around you?**

- **What is God calling you to do in light of our time at Caesarea by the Sea?**

- **What direction do you think He wants you to go next?**

Pray

Jesus,

You don't wait for perfect people; You launch willing ones.

You took a man who broke things and made him into a man who built churches, who carried love like fire in his bones. You used Caesarea—a city Paul didn't choose—as a launching point to change the world.

We don't want to waste the places we didn't choose either. So here we are, God, standing on our own launchpads. Maybe it's a hospital room. Maybe it's a cubicle. Maybe it's a kitchen table.

But You're with us. And You're whispering through the headset like our own personal capcom: "You're ready. I'm with you. This is your moment."

Give us the courage to lift off—to love first, speak when it's time, and live like Love when it's better to show than shout.

We don't need a title or a platform, just a fast horse. Maybe it's a story, a meal, a phone call, or a moment of inexplicable kindness. Remind us that love doesn't have to be loud—it just has to be real.

Jesus, help us love like You love. Help us see people the way You did from the rooftop in Joppa. Help us break down the lines we've drawn around faith circles. Let our hearts be wider than our theology sometimes, because You always made more room for more people, not less.

And when we're afraid of what's next, remind us: You're already there.

So give us fire, give us peace, give us joy that doesn't depend on the outcome. And let our lives, our actual lives, tell the story. Not a sermon, not a sales pitch. Just love. Bold, winsome, wild, Jesus-style love.

In Your name, amen.

Extend Your Stay

If you want to spend a little more time at this stop, scan the QR code here (access code: Journey). You can take a tour through Caesarea by the Sea, download a digital recipe, and find cool links.

Recipe

Limonana

(ISRAELI MINT LEMONADE)

In Caesarea by the Sea, I discovered that there is nothing better on a warm Mediterranean afternoon than limonana. Modern-day Caesarea by the Sea is dotted with kosher cafés and beachside bars where you'll find limonana being served to locals and tourists alike.

You know what I love about limonana? It's both sweet and tart, and it's got this little twist of mint to wake you up just a bit. Isn't that what Jesus does in places like this? He shakes us awake.

Caesarea is more than ruins; it's also a reminder. This was the place where power strutted around in a palace and God whispered hope through a prisoner in chains. Paul was here. Pilate was here. Herod built things here. God built the church here.

And maybe, just maybe, God's message for you today as you or your Bible study group enjoy a glass of limonana is this: Stay sweet, stay sharp, and stay refreshing. Like limonana.

YOU WILL NEED:

1 cup fresh lemon juice (about 4–6 lemons)
½ cup fresh mint leaves
½–¾ cup sugar or honey (to taste)
4 cups cold water (or half water, half sparkling water), divided
Ice cubes
Sprigs of mint, for garnish

DIRECTIONS:

1. Blend lemon juice, mint, sugar, and 1 cup of water until smooth.
2. Strain into a pitcher.
3. Stir in remaining water.
4. Serve over ice and garnish with a sprig of mint.

Multiply this recipe according to the size of your group if you're sharing.*

*Based on a recipe from https://toriavey.com/limonana-frozen-mint-lemonade.

Mount of Beatitudes

STOP 6

WALKING WITH IMAGINATION AT THE MOUNT OF BEATITUDES

Bob's Travel Log

I'm so far up on the Mount of Beatitudes that I feel like I could touch heaven. It was here in this very spot that Jesus sat down, looked out at the people He loved, and told them the upside-down truths of His kingdom.

As I pause to listen, I hear the wind coming off the Sea of Galilee just down the hill. The birds are doing their thing, the wildflowers are dancing in the breeze, and honestly, it feels like the whole earth is holding its breath to hear the words again: "Blessed are the poor in spirit ... the meek ... the merciful ... the pure in heart."

This wasn't just a sermon; it was a revolution. Jesus wasn't handing out motivational quotes; He was flipping the script on everything we thought we knew. It was as if He was saying, "You want to be first? Be last. You want to be great? Get low. You want the kingdom? Come empty."

I imagine the crowd wasn't expecting that. People came looking for a king to crush their enemies, and they got a carpenter who blessed the broken. That's what I love about Jesus—He never plays by the world's rules, because He has a heavenly agenda, and I thank God for that.

I can picture Jesus pointing across the landscape at a nearby city and saying, "You are the salt of the earth ... the light of the world ... a city on a hill" (see Matt. 5:13–14).

He didn't say, "Try to be" those things. He said, "You *are*." Right here on this hillside, Jesus looked at people who probably didn't feel very shiny or salty, and He told them they already were. He gave them an identity.

Really, that's what Jesus is still doing. He's not asking us to earn His light inside us or prove that we have it. He's asking us to live like it's true. But sometimes, we get so busy trying to climb ladders and make names for ourselves that we miss the voice of God whispering over the birds, the flowers, and His people, saying, "You're already mine. You're already blessed."

I want to sit on the hillside with Jesus. To stop trying to be impressive and start being present.

May we leave this place a little saltier, shine a little brighter, and love a whole lot deeper.

It's time to watch the video for this stop.
Settle in for a few minutes and scan the QR code (access code: Journey).

Drop a Pin

- **Where are you right now in relation to what I spoke about in this section's video? Excited? Curious? Lost? Jot down your thoughts in the space below.**

DISCOVERING GOD'S UPSIDE-DOWN KINGDOM AT THE MOUNT OF BEATITUDES

Read Your Map

Now when Jesus saw the crowds, he went up on a mountainside and sat down. His disciples came to him, and he began to teach them.

He said:

"Blessed are the poor in spirit,
for theirs is the kingdom of heaven.
Blessed are those who mourn,
for they will be comforted.
Blessed are the meek,
for they will inherit the earth.
Blessed are those who hunger and thirst for righteousness,
for they will be filled.
Blessed are the merciful,
for they will be shown mercy.
Blessed are the pure in heart,
for they will see God.

> Blessed are the peacemakers,
> for they will be called children of God.
> Blessed are those who are persecuted because of righteousness,
> for theirs is the kingdom of heaven.
>
> Blessed are you when people insult you, persecute you and falsely say all kinds of evil against you because of me. Rejoice and be glad, because great is your reward in heaven, for in the same way they persecuted the prophets who were before you." (Matt. 5:1–12)

Here's the truth: Jesus didn't come to improve our lives a little; He came to flip everything upside down.

I don't know about you, but when I'm mourning the loss of a loved one or a dream that's fallen through or a relationship that has dissolved, I don't exactly jump to the thought that that circumstance is a blessing. I tend to call instances like that a burden. However, on this hillside, Jesus invites us to a kingdom where the low are lifted and the mourners are honored. And in every instance where we might feel burdened, Jesus called us blessed.

The Greek word for "blessed" is *makarios,* which means "happy." But this isn't like the happy you feel when you take your first bite of your favorite pizza. This happy is a God happy. It's a joy that is, as Scottish theologian and minister William Barclay put it, "untouchable, and self-contained, that joy which is completely independent of all the chances and changes of life."[1]

The reality is that upside-down blessings (those things we call burdens) shape our lives in remarkable ways.

For twenty years, I built a lodge. One day, it caught fire and burned to the ground in just twenty minutes. Twenty years of work gone in twenty minutes. Can you believe that? It wasn't just the loss of that wonderful home that was devastating; it was that everything we owned, including photographs and family mementos, was turned to ash. It was bad. Really, really bad. Sweet Maria, our family, and I took about a year to grieve. And then we realized we had a strong vision for this project. We couldn't give up. For the next four years, we rebuilt the lodge.

What was wild was that, while processing this incident through counseling, my wife was able to uncover some trauma that had been buried in her past. It took our dreams going up in flames for her to heal. If I had known what would come from all that rubble, maybe I would have lit the match myself.

Hopefully, for you, it wasn't a house that burned down. But you've seen some of your own blessings turn to burdens. A relationship went sour. You took a career leap that led to a fall. Whatever it was, we've all experienced this blessing-to-burden shift. And there's something beautiful that happens here in the hardship that we'll miss if we zero in on our struggle.

God uses suffering to draw close to us, move on our behalf, and shape us more into His image. Tragedy exposes our great need for God[2] and allows us to reestablish our foundation on Him if we've built it on something wobbly like our own pride or material possessions.

- **Read Romans 5:3–5. What do these verses say that suffering produces in us?**

Here's the big takeaway I've learned through the Beatitudes and life experience: If you want a different outcome, the first step is to adopt a different outlook.

Don't get me wrong. I'm not saying to ignore the hurt or pain you feel. That's like standing at the edge of the ocean and trying to hold back the tide. Inevitably, the reality of life's problems will wash over us. But when it does, we get to decide if we're going to let the tide push us toward God or pull us under the weight of our issues. We can determine whether we see ourselves as blessed or burdened. We can expect God to rebuild something incredible in our lives, or we can stand in the ash with a woe-is-me attitude.

Take a look at Romans 8:28 and fill in the blank:

> And we know that in all things God works for the ____________________ of those who love him, who have been called according to his purpose.

What if we caught enough whimsy to believe this verse was always true in our lives? If we embraced the mystery of why bad things happen? If we decided to feel the pain but also focus on its purpose and trust that God really is up to some good in our lives?

Group Discussion Prompt

- Which beatitude do you need most today?
- How does this "reverse economy" challenge how you typically understand burdens and blessings?

It's particularly interesting to note that Jesus said, "Blessed *are*," not "Blessed will eventually be." This means that in this present moment, Jesus sees us as blessed. The joy we long for isn't on the other side of our problems; it's right in the middle because that's where Jesus is too.

What if, today, right here at the Mount of Beatitudes, we decided to be treasure hunters? When life starts pressing in, we can explore the depths of our pain and discover what God is up to. Is there a sunken treasure He wants us to discover at the bottom of that problem? Is there a wealth of wisdom that hardship is producing in us? Are all the squishy sides of our faith becoming stronger because of the workout life is putting us through?

We find our joy by diving in and discovering that the greatest treasure is that God's kingdom is completely upside-down.

Drop a Pin

- **Write down one area where you feel poor in spirit or overlooked. Ask God to show you how He's already blessing that very place.**

BIRDS, LILIES, AND A KINGDOM WITHOUT WORRY

Read Your Map

Therefore I tell you, do not worry about your life, what you will eat or drink; or about your body, what you will wear. Is not life more than food, and the body

> more than clothes? Look at the birds of the air; they do not sow or reap or store away in barns, and yet your heavenly Father feeds them. Are you not much more valuable than they? Can any one of you by worrying add a single hour to your life?
>
> And why do you worry about clothes? See how the flowers of the field grow. They do not labor or spin. Yet I tell you that not even Solomon in all his splendor was dressed like one of these. If that is how God clothes the grass of the field, which is here today and tomorrow is thrown into the fire, will he not much more clothe you—you of little faith? So do not worry, saying, "What shall we eat?" or "What shall we drink?" or "What shall we wear?" For the pagans run after all these things, and your heavenly Father knows that you need them. But seek first his kingdom and his righteousness, and all these things will be given to you as well. Therefore do not worry about tomorrow, for tomorrow will worry about itself. Each day has enough trouble of its own. (Matt. 6:25–34)

On the Mount of Beatitudes, Jesus didn't just teach about blessing; He went on to tie His upside-down kingdom to the concept of trust. What He knew, which I think we all know somewhere deep inside our hearts, is that worry doesn't ever get us where we want to go. But trust in God does.

The Anxiety & Depression Association of America did a study recently and discovered that over 40 percent of Americans are more stressed out than the year before. The study also found that nearly forty million adults have a clinically diagnosed anxiety disorder.[3] That's a lot of people! That means that for every five people standing in line at your local coffee shop, at least one of them is struggling significantly with anxiety.

Worry and anxiety are quite the epidemic here in America. You'd think that with all our gadgets and apps and smart appliances, our lives would be getting less stressful. But the opposite seems to be happening. I think what all these things really offer us is a false sense of control.

Have you ever ordered anything on Amazon? I have the Amazon app, and after I've bought a new shirt or something fun, I check my orders tab several times to see just when my new purchases are going to come in. I can't actually control when those packages arrive, but the app makes me feel like I can a little bit. Like, maybe if I check it again, it'll get here a little quicker. Oh, now it's out for delivery. Hey, it's here, just like I knew it would be!

Group Discussion Prompt

- Why do you think trusting God is so hard to do sometimes?
- What are you most tempted to worry about?

Social media lets us think we can control the perception people have of our lives by allowing us to post only our highlight reels. Having grocery stores stocked with all our favorite foods gives us a sense of control over our diet. We can even set the temperature inside our homes so we have no surprises about how hot or cold it is. We think we know what, who, where, how, and when to expect something.

The reality is that we have very little control over anything. Social media could crash. Amazon could go away. Our air conditioner could go out at any moment.

These are all minor examples. But there are major ones too. Like not being able to make decisions for our spouses or friends when we think we know what's best for them. Or wanting to put our children in a bubble where nothing can hurt them but having to release them out into the world to make their own mistakes.

What does God ask us to do with the things we worry about and want to control? Trust Him.

Take a moment to read the following psalms and proverb and write down what they say about trusting God.

- Psalm 9:10
- Psalm 28:7
- Psalm 37:4–6
- Proverbs 3:5

Let's get back to the birds and the lilies in our main passage. Jesus said:

> Look at the birds of the air; they do not sow or reap or store away in barns, and yet your heavenly Father feeds them....

> And why do you worry about clothes? See how the flowers of the field grow. They do not labor or spin. Yet I tell you that not even Solomon in all his splendor was dressed like one of these. If that is how God clothes the grass of the field, which is here today and tomorrow is thrown into the fire, will he not much more clothe you—you of little faith? (Matt. 6:26a, 28–30)

If you've ever gone out in nature to notice the birds and the flowers, perhaps you've observed that they don't worry. However, collecting their food and clothing does require work. Birds rise early to catch those worms. Bees and butterflies pollinate flowers. Gardeners plant seeds and water them to help them grow.

Combating our own worries may also take work. Here's a way I've found to tackle my own anxieties. First, figure out what your worry stems from. Are you scared you won't be provided for? Has life taught you that you could be abandoned, so you believe God might leave you high and dry as well? Have you had to be fiercely independent, so you think that if you need something, you'll have to make it happen?

After figuring out the root of your worry, break down what you have control over and what you don't. Let go of the longing to influence the outcome of every single thing in your life. Take courageous steps to steward well what you can control. Stop trying to control what you can't. And trust God with both. When Jesus says, "Therefore do not worry," He's saying to replace that worry with the work it takes to focus on the upside-down kingdom of God.

When I'm looking for God's heart and am focused on things that have heavenly value, I zero in less on materialistic things and end up finding what's best for me and those around me.

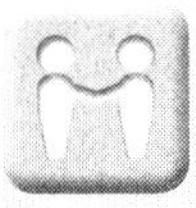

Find Your Friends

One time, I read a children's book about buckets, and it shifted my whole perspective. The premise of the book was that we become what we fill our lives (buckets) with.

I decided to take this book very literally and bought a galvanized bucket with an aluminum handle to carry with me everywhere I went. As I got into cars, headed out for a sail, or switched trains on the subway, I probably looked like a dairy farmer who'd lost his way. Yes, I looked silly. But it was a constant reminder to fill my bucket with God things instead of Bob junk.

If we fill our buckets with worry, we'll become worriers. If we fill it with trust in God, we will not only become more aware of our blessings but also understand trust better and be able to share that with others. Trusting God can teach us how to become trustworthy people.

- **Who is someone you can trust?**

- **What would it look like for you to love others well by being a trustworthy friend?**

- **What are you filling your bucket with, and how do you think that overflows onto others?**

Matthew 6 concludes with Jesus telling us to not worry about tomorrow because today has enough trouble on its own. This is hard to grasp in a society that is so future focused. As we near the end of high school, we're asked what we we're going to do next. Couples who just got married are met with questions of when they're going to have kids. People say it's wise to make a five-year plan.

Listen, I love a good plan. I help people from all over plan things like how to share their stories or get where they feel led to go. But sometimes I think we can get so future focused that we miss the ground right under our feet.

Look up 1 Peter 5:7 and fill in the blanks:

Cast all your ______________________________ on him because he ______________________________ for you.

We get to show up in the present and take life one day at a time because Jesus set us free from having to control everything. He holds the world in the palm of His hand. And He deeply cares about our future.

So keep planning the future and recalling the past, but live in and for the present.

Drop a Pin

- **What does it look like to trust God more than your own plans? When it comes to worrying, what do you need to work through? What does it mean that God cares for the lilies and birds and He cares even more for you?**

BUILDING A LIFE LIKE A WISE MAN, NOT A SANDMAN

Read Your Map

> Therefore everyone who hears these words of mine and puts them into practice is like a wise man who built his house on the rock. The rain came down, the streams rose, and the winds blew and beat against that house; yet it did not fall, because it had its foundation on the rock. But everyone who hears these words of mine and does not put them into practice is like a

> foolish man who built his house on sand. The rain came down, the streams rose, and the winds blew and beat against that house, and it fell with a great crash. (Matt. 7:24–27)

On the Mount of Beatitudes, we've learned a lot about what Jesus said. In Matthew 7, we see His call to put His words into action.

Every day, whether we pay much attention to it or not, we're building a life. We ultimately get to choose what we build. Will we put up walls that push people out or create open doors to let them in? Will we make God's Word our solid foundation, or will we build on something less sound, like our own opinions or the thoughts of others? Will we paint everything with our complaints and hardships or splash the halls with colorful banners that tell of our best memories? Will the structure we build reflect our focus on ourselves or have long tables and many chairs to create a safe space for others?

Here in Matthew 7, Jesus gives us a peek at two different builders. Each man's house looked pretty much the same on the outside. I'm sure they were nice. For our discussion, let's say they were welcoming, functional homes like Craftsman bungalows. I like those because they're so rich in character and have cozy communal spaces. They normally have front porches that say, "Sit and stay awhile."

So these men both built Craftsman bungalows but built them on different foundations. One chose the beachfront (can you blame him?), while the other chose a rocky outcrop. Now, at first glance we probably all would have looked at the guy putting his bungalow on the rocks and thought he was missing out. Why live in the rocks when you can chill by the shore?

But then the rain fell, the floods rose, and the winds blew. Back when Jesus shared this message, there were no bombs or armed drones. Storms caused more disaster than anything else, and they were often thought of as a way God carried out His judgment on the earth.

The illustration Jesus was offering to the people gathered on the Mount of Beatitudes was of a great shaking. He wasn't alluding to minor struggles like not wanting to do chores on their farms because they are hard. He was talking about when life completely slams into you. There's a great loss in the family. Financial issues skyrocket. Health plummets. Tragedy strikes.

Life's storms reveal our hidden foundations by showing us what is (or is not) still standing when the shaking subsides.

- **Look up Proverbs 10:25. This verse was written just over a thousand years before the book of Matthew. How does it compare to Jesus' teaching? Do you think it's possible He could have been referring to this Old Testament passage?**

The mistake for the second builder was that he didn't consider his foundation. How many times do we do this too? We go about our days, building our lives, and we don't even pay attention to what we're constructing our thoughts, actions, and intentions on. To change this, we have to adopt the wise-man approach, not the sandman approach. We have to be intentional about our foundation.

Jesus concludes this section with a warning. He says, "But everyone who hears these words of mine and does not put them into practice is like a foolish man who built his house on sand. The rain came down, the streams rose, and the winds blew and beat against that house, and it fell with a great crash" (Matt. 7:26–27).

Clearly, sitting in church, listening to our favorite Christian podcasts, or turning on some worship music in our car isn't enough to establish a strong foundation. They're more like the framing of the life we're building, helping us hold up our godly intentions.

- **Read James 1:22. What does this verse command us to do?**

Group Discussion Prompt

Making God's Word the foundation for your life choices can seem like an intimidating decision. That's why I have decided to follow Jesus just thirty seconds at a time. Because life isn't just one big decision; it's a million tiny ongoing choices.

Changing my entire life feels really hard, but simply doing the next kind thing doesn't. I can easily take thirty seconds to look at my feet, see where they are planted, and decide to be fully present in that place. I even like taking several minutes to create a whimsical surprise for a friend, like sending them balloons and a note on a random Tuesday. It doesn't take but a second to say a quick prayer and hear from God in a way that might change the trajectory of my entire day.

- Does making God the foundation of your life seem intimidating? Why do you think that is?
- Is it easier to think about following Jesus thirty seconds at a time? What would implementing this in your own life look like? What would it look like within your church, community, and family?

Have you ever heard the phrase "Doing nothing is still deciding to do something"? It's true in this case. We can hear all the popular sermons on YouTube and sing all the worship songs that made it to the top of our Spotify lists, but if we aren't doers of the Word, we're no different from the sandman who built a pretty life without a firm foundation. So how *do* we construct a life on a strong foundation like the wise man and avoid catastrophe when the storms of life billow our way?

Look at the following chart and fill in what being a wise person looks like for you:

Principle	Insight	Bible Reference	Personal Application
Be a doer.	Obey God 30 seconds at a time.	Matthew 7:24	
Actively love others.	Loving others is the greatest command and a great first action step when we don't know what God wants us to do.	Matthew 22:38	
Fail forward.	Failure is a part of the building process.	1 John 1:8-9	

Listen, we're going to make mistakes on our faith journey. But we can decide to "fail forward." Confessing our sins actually clears the way for a sturdier foundation. Each time we come to God and say, "Hey, I really messed up here," He's able to cover our mistakes with grace and offer us some better building material. Failing forward is exchanging sand for the Rock.

- **Let's wrap this up by looking at three verses in 2 Samuel 22. What do verses 2, 32, and 47 refer to God as?**

Thankfully, a rock-solid life doesn't depend on us. God is our Rock, so we don't have to be. When life shakes, He doesn't. Allowing God to be the foundation of our wild, wonderful lives means that, through all the ups and downs, our joy, zeal, courageous curiosity, and hope are as immovable as the Rock we stand on.

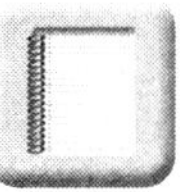

Personal Travel Log

Reach deep. At the Mount of Beatitudes, we learned that Jesus introduced an upside-down kingdom. He called the poor in spirit, the mourners, the meek, the peacemakers, and the persecuted "blessed"—not because their circumstances were easy but because God was near. This teaching invites us to see hardship as the fertile ground for transformation. Blessing, in Jesus' eyes, is found not after the pain ends but in the messy middle of it.

Jesus also challenged us to live in the present, not preoccupied with tomorrow, and to build our lives on His words like a wise builder building on solid rock. This means doing the next kind thing, showing up where our feet are, and letting our faith be active and rooted in obedience. Our lives don't have to be perfect to be strong; they just need the right foundation. And the good news is that God doesn't ask us to be the rock—He is.

God is sending us from the Mount of Beatitudes, asking us to build a strong foundation and live out what we believe.

As you reflect on what you just learned, consider these questions:

- **Where do you now see that you have been building your house on the sand instead of the Rock?**

- **What is your key takeaway from this section?**

- **Where do you see God at work in your life and in the lives of others around you?**

- **What is God calling you to do in light of our time at the Mount of Beatitudes?**

- **What direction do you think He wants you to go next?**

Pray

God,

Thanks for meeting us here on this hillside to remind us that You didn't come with a list of rules or a five-step program. You told us we were blessed. *Right now. Right here. Just as we are.*

Thanks for revealing Your upside-down kingdom where the poor are rich, the mourning are comforted, and the meek are strong. That's not how the world works, but it's how Your kingdom works. I need help seeing that sometimes. When all I can see are ashes, remind me that You are planting something new.

God, I don't want to just hear Your words; I want to *do* them. Show me how to build my life on the Rock, thirty seconds at a time. Help me trust You with the stuff I can't control and start looking at the birds and the lilies again. I want to be someone who withstands the storms of life, not because I'm strong, but because I'm standing on You.

Help me fill my bucket with trust, not fear. With love, not control. And if I mess it up today (which I probably will), remind me that You're not disappointed—You're just ready to help me rebuild.

I love You. I trust You. And I'm really glad You're not finished with me yet.

In Jesus' name, amen.

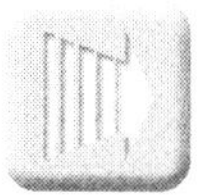

Extend Your Stay

If you want to spend a little more time at this stop, scan the QR code here (access code: Journey). You can take a tour through the Mount of Beatitudes, download a digital recipe, and find cool links.

Recipe

Za'atar Pita Chips with Olive Oil

Now that we've dived into the Beatitudes, I want to share a recipe for something I think Jesus would've passed around on that hillside if He could have: za'atar pita chips with olive oil. This is a region where olives thrive, so their oil is a fundamental ingredient in most foods here, including this snack. It's simple, but adding the za'atar—made of local herbs like thyme, sumac, and sesame seeds—kicks the flavor up a notch. These chips are perfectly crunchy, salty, and earthy.

Here's what else I love about these little pita chips: They remind us that simple can be sacred, and humble can be holy. They don't need a fancy dish or a perfect kitchen. Just a willing heart and a little heat.

Make these at home. Bring them to your neighbors. Pass them around at your next Bible study. And when you do, remember: Jesus fed people with bread and truth. This snack offers an opportunity to gather around both.

So crunch away, friends!

YOU WILL NEED:

4 pieces pita bread, or flatbread
2–3 tablespoons extra-virgin olive oil
2–3 tablespoons za'atar, or a mix of thyme, oregano, sumac, sesame seeds, and salt
Pinch of sea salt
Hummus, for serving (optional)

DIRECTIONS:

1. Preheat oven to 375°F.
2. Slice pita bread into triangles or strips.
3. Brush or drizzle olive oil over the pita pieces.

4. Sprinkle generously with za'atar and sea salt.
5. Bake for 8–10 minutes, or until golden and crisp.
6. Cool slightly and enjoy plain or with hummus.

Multiply the recipe according to how many people you're sharing it with. Enjoy loudly!*

*Based on a recipe from https://reformjudaism.org/reform-jewish-life/food-recipes/homemade-pita-chips-zaatar.

The Valley of Elah

STOP 7

THROWING FRIENDSHIPS AT GIANTS IN THE VALLEY OF ELAH

Bob's Travel Log

As I stand on the dusty rolling hills in the Valley of Elah, the breeze lightly blows through the barley fields and olive trees. The rocks underfoot are smooth. I think if I listen hard enough, I can almost hear a teenage shepherd talking back to a giant.

As I overlook this valley, I can picture that young shepherd, David, looking at the Israelites shaking in their sandals while they stare at a nine-foot-nine-inch giant who has been taunting them for days. He saw what I also see: God is in this place. Even in their fear, God was on their side.

This makes me wonder: What giants have I let stand too long in my life—just because I forgot that God was standing with me?

There is a dry riverbed here that still holds smooth stones like the ones David would have chosen for his sling to hurl at Goliath. Those worn-down rocks remind me that faith has never been flashy. It's sometimes just one foot in front of the other, one smooth stone in a sling, one voice confidently saying, "I come in the name of the Lord."

David didn't win because he was brave. He defeated the giant because he believed. He knew God wasn't just with him but also already out there on the battlefield. It was God's fight to win, not his.

So today, I picked up a stone from the Valley of Elah because, like David, I want to remember who's fighting for us and that the battle belongs to Him. Sometimes the odds seem stacked against us, but now, after visiting this spot, I know for certain that the God of David still meets people in valleys, slays giants, and offers us victory when we call upon His name.

It's time to watch the video for this stop.
Settle in for a few minutes and scan the QR code (access code: Journey).

Drop a Pin

- **Where are you right now in relation to what I spoke about in this section's video? Excited? Curious? Lost? Jot down your thoughts in the space below.**

FACING GIANTS IN THE VALLEY OF ELAH

Read Your Map

> Now the Philistines gathered their forces for war and assembled at Sokoh in Judah. They pitched camp at Ephes Dammim, between Sokoh and Azekah. Saul and the Israelites assembled and camped in the Valley of Elah and drew up their battle line to meet the Philistines. The Philistines occupied one hill and the Israelites another, with the valley between them.
>
> A champion named Goliath, who was from Gath, came out of the Philistine camp. His height was six cubits and a span. He had a bronze helmet on his head and wore a coat of scale armor of bronze weighing five thousand shekels; on his legs he wore bronze greaves, and a bronze javelin was slung on his back. His spear shaft was like a weaver's rod, and its iron point weighed six hundred shekels. His shield bearer went ahead of him.
>
> Goliath stood and shouted to the ranks of Israel, "Why do you come out and line up for battle? Am I not a Philistine, and are you not the servants of Saul? Choose a man and have him come down to me. If he is able to fight and kill me, we will become your subjects; but if I overcome him and kill him, you will become our subjects and serve us." Then the Philistine said, "This day I defy the armies of Israel! Give me a man and let us fight each other." On hearing the Philistine's words, Saul and all the Israelites were dismayed and terrified....
>
> For forty days the Philistine came forward every morning and evening and took his stand. (1 Sam. 17:1–11, 16)

Welcome to the Valley of Elah. This beautiful spot was a battlefield where, with five smooth stones and a sling, the shepherd boy David faced down a giant who was believed to be over nine feet tall ("six cubits and a span"). When you read his description in our key passage, it's no wonder the Israelites were intimidated. This warrior was the Incredible Hulk for the Philistines.

At this time in history, around 1012 BC, the Philistines were enemies of Israel.[1] Their feud began as they argued over who rightfully owned the land of Israel. Adding to the tensions between them, the Philistines did what they could to prevent Israel from having access to their resources.[2]

- **Take a look at 1 Samuel 13:19–22. What did the Philistines withhold from the Israelites? What problem did this create?**

While the Philistines were incredibly powerful, they had one huge thing working against them: They didn't worship the one true God. Instead, they worshipped what I like to call a bunch of "little-*g* gods" like Dagon (1 Sam. 5:2–5) and Baal (2 Kings 1:2–3). So the God of Israel was not on their side as they invaded through the Valley of Elah, some twenty-five miles southwest of Jerusalem.

This is how we get to the battle in the Valley of Elah. Saul, king of the Israelites, couldn't let the Philistines conquer his land. So he and the Israelite army lined up on one side of the valley, and the Philistines drew up on the opposite side.

Take another look at 1 Samuel 17:8–9 and fill in the blanks:

> Goliath stood and shouted to the ranks of Israel, "Why do you come out and line up for battle? Am I not a Philistine, and are you not the servants of Saul? Choose a man and have him come down to me. If he is able to fight and kill me, we will ______________________________
> ______________________________;
> but if I overcome him and kill him, you will become ______________
> ______________________________."

Goliath set the stakes pretty high for this fight, didn't he? It was a winner-takes-all kind of battle, and Goliath threw this threat in the Israelites' faces for quite a while.

- **Glance back at 1 Samuel 17:16. How many days did Goliath taunt the Israelites?**

Biblical numerology is so fascinating that some people dedicate their lives to studying it. Here's what some have discovered about the number forty in the Bible: It usually represents a time of trial or testing or signifies God's judgment.[3]

Look up the following verses and write what you discover about the number forty:

- Genesis 7:4
- Exodus 16:35
- Judges 13:1
- 1 Samuel 4:18
- 2 Samuel 5:4
- Matthew 4:2
- Luke 4:2
- Acts 1:3

David, a shepherd boy who had fought off lions and bears while herding vulnerable sheep, was

Group Discussion Prompt

The clearest memory I have of shaking in my boots was at the beginning of law school. During orientation, one of the faculty members had given us an incredibly un-peppy pep talk, saying that one-third of the class was bound to flunk out. I turned to count the chairs to find which one I was sitting in. No matter which direction I counted, I was in the third chair. The giant of fear told me I wasn't going to make it. It drove me to have thoughts about quitting law school altogether.

Because that's what giants make us want to do—back down and quit. In these instances, we are tempted to settle for quivering on the sidelines like the rest of the Israelites, but if we do, we may never find out what victory looks like.

- What is the giant in your life right now?
- Is it calling you out and making you want to shrink back?
- How does your giant's taunting differ from the words God speaks over you?
- How can we, as a community of faith, help each other slay our giants?

certainly not new to testing and trials. I'm sure those sheep tested his patience as they wandered away. Fighting off predators was probably second nature to him. While the army of Israel cowered for forty days, David saw this trial as an opportunity for God to triumph over His enemies.

When giants step into the valleys of our lives, we too have a choice. We can shake in our boots on the sidelines or fight from the victory that we already know is ours in Christ.

What if, instead of avoiding our giants, we (like David) confront them? When we name our giants, we begin to understand what's really going on, and our giants seemingly begin to shrink.

Listen, I know your "giant" probably doesn't carry a javelin the size of a fence post, so whatever is standing against you might not seem as dangerous as Goliath. However, it has been shouting you down day after day, telling you that you should be afraid of the future, that you're not enough, that you don't have anything to offer, and that you're not worthy of a win. But here's the secret ...

The real giant slayer isn't you—it's God. David was a kid! He wasn't the biggest or strongest man in the army. But he knew that God stood with him and that God would lead His people to victory.

In the same way, we don't have to be brutal enough to face our giants alone. We don't have to be strong enough to hit our hardships with enough force to deliver a KO. We don't have to muster up our strength and white-knuckle it through the valleys of our lives. We can face our giants, call them by name, and allow God to step into the ring with us and fight on our behalf until He is declared the victor.

Drop a Pin

- **Today you faced your giant in the Valley of Elah. How did it feel? What was your giant's name?**

- **How can you look your giant in the eye and ask God to fight for you?**

IN THE FIGHT OF YOUR LIFE, USE WHAT YOU'VE GOT

Read Your Map

> David said to Saul, "Let no one lose heart on account of this Philistine; your servant will go and fight him."
>
> Saul replied, "You are not able to go out against this Philistine and fight him; you are only a young man, and he has been a warrior from his youth."
>
> But David said to Saul, "Your servant has been keeping his father's sheep. When a lion or a bear came and carried off a sheep from the flock, I went after it, struck it and rescued the sheep from its mouth. When it turned on me, I seized it by its hair, struck it and killed it. Your servant has killed both the lion and the bear; this uncircumcised Philistine will be like one of them, because he has defied the armies of the living God. The LORD who rescued me from the paw of the lion and the paw of the bear will rescue me from the hand of this Philistine."
>
> Saul said to David, "Go, and the LORD be with you."
>
> Then Saul dressed David in his own tunic. He put a coat of armor on him and a bronze helmet on his head. David fastened on his sword over the tunic and tried walking around, because he was not used to them.
>
> "I cannot go in these," he said to Saul, "because I am not used to them." So he took them off. Then he took his staff in his hand, chose five smooth stones from the stream, put them in the pouch of his shepherd's bag and, with his sling in his hand, approached the Philistine. (1 Sam. 17:32–40)

When someone asks for advice, what they really want is your experience. For example, I've sailed across the ocean several times. I'm not sure why I keep doing this, because I usually fight seasickness the whole way. But there's something about me that loves the adventure and the open sea.

Whenever I'm about to embark on these expeditions, I always receive unsolicited advice from people. One time, a guy who heard I was heading out on a sailing trip decided to offer me directions, a packing list, and all kinds of tips. So I asked him, "Oh, are you a sailor?" His shocking reply was "I've never left Ohio."

In our Bible passage, David experienced the same thing. Saul and his men offered David a lot of advice. Saul even gave David his armor. The issue was that while they had a ton of experience as warriors, David didn't. He had never even worn armor. I imagine his awkward teenage body clanging around in oversized metal and him thinking, *This is definitely not going to work.*

Instead of trying to go into battle in ways he hadn't tried, David leaned into his own experience. He didn't know anything about armor or swords, but he knew very well how to turn a stone into a lethal projectile with a sling. David's shepherding background was no accident. His unique training in the field had perfectly equipped him to defeat Goliath on the field of battle.

Maybe David was taking notes from one of the fathers of his faith, Moses.

- **Look up Exodus 4:2. As Moses is asking for God to show up in a miraculous way in front of his enemies, what does God ask him?**

Moses had a simple staff in his hand, a piece of wood that God used to perform signs and wonders. God used that stick to part the entire Red Sea, for crying out loud. Similarly, God used a simple slingshot in the hands of a shepherd boy to defeat a giant. David knew what God had put into his hand, and he used it.

Group Discussion Prompt

God isn't asking you to be someone you're not. He's interested in what you already have in your hand. What's the gift you've been practicing in private? What grit have you been building in the field of life?

In light of this, answer these questions with your group:

- In what ways have you seen God uniquely equip people for a battle they had to endure? How have you seen this play out in your own life?
- What keeps us from using our tools and talents for God?
- What would it look like for you to step onto the battlefield to fight for others using your talents?

What about you? God has been shaping a weapon in your hand to fight back against the giants that taunt and paralyze you. It might not look like much—but in God's hands, it's a powerful tool.

Walk in what you've already been trained in. Because what we learn from David is this: You can't win your battle in someone else's armor.

Do you ever catch yourself wishing for someone else's armor? I know I do. There are times I start pursuing someone else's version of success instead of what I know God is asking me to do. You know what happens every time? I start to believe that I'm second-rate and not even worthy to step out into the battle. Someone else out there would be a better pick than me. And I miss out. There could have been a God-sized win in my life, but I pre-decided that I was a loser compared to that other guy over there, so I never even got in the game.

- **Read Romans 12:5–8. In your own words, what does this say about our unique giftings?**

- **How do David's actions in 1 Samuel 17 compare to this New Testament teaching?**

Here's something awesome I've learned about God: He never wastes anything. The unique talents and skills we have developed through the hardships of life are actually our secret weapons for slaying the giants that will come against us.

So take a good look at what you have in your hand. It may seem normal, ordinary, or simple. But in the hands of a mighty God, our tools and life experiences are extraordinary. He used a shepherd boy with a sling to slay a giant. What do you think He could do through you if you stepped into the fight for your life willing to give Him your gifts for His glory?

Drop a Pin

- **Take a moment to reflect on what unique talents and tools God has placed in your hand. What are they? Write them down. Beside each tool, brainstorm how God could use it to cause giants to fall in your life and the lives of others.**

THROWING FRIENDSHIPS AT GIANTS

Read Your Map

Meanwhile, the Philistine, with his shield bearer in front of him, kept coming closer to David. He looked David over and saw that he was little more than a boy, glowing with health and handsome, and he despised him. He said to David, "Am I a dog, that you come at me with sticks?" And the Philistine cursed David by his gods. "Come here," he said, "and I'll give your flesh to the birds and the wild animals!"

David said to the Philistine, "You come against me with sword and spear and javelin, but I come against you in the name of the LORD Almighty, the God of the armies of Israel, whom you have defied. This day the LORD will deliver you into my hands, and I'll strike you down and cut off your head. This very day I will give the carcasses of the Philistine army to the birds and the wild animals, and the whole world will know that there is a God in Israel. All those gathered here will know that it is not by sword or spear that the LORD saves; for the battle is the LORD's, and he will give all of you into our hands."

As the Philistine moved closer to attack him, David ran quickly toward the battle line to meet him. Reaching into his bag and taking out a stone, he slung

> it and struck the Philistine on the forehead. The stone sank into his forehead, and he fell facedown on the ground.
>
> So David triumphed over the Philistine with a sling and a stone; without a sword in his hand he struck down the Philistine and killed him.
>
> David ran and stood over him. He took hold of the Philistine's sword and drew it from the sheath. After he killed him, he cut off his head with the sword.
>
> When the Philistines saw that their hero was dead, they turned and ran. (1 Sam. 17:41–51)

Unlike the rest of the Israelite army, David didn't just hope and pray that the giant would go away. He ran toward Goliath into what looked like an unfair fight. Goliath was so much bigger than David that, if you review 1 Samuel 17:41–43, Goliath seemed to have to get a little closer to David to even notice his features. When he realized David was just a boy, Goliath was insulted. Certainly, he deserved to fight Israel's best warrior, but there was no way this kid was it. His pride shattered, Goliath rained down insults on David, and he stepped in to fight the kid.

To those on the battlefield sidelines, it must have seemed like this battle was between a nine-foot-nine-inch giant (with his armor bearer lurking nearby) and a solo shepherd boy. To the Philistines, it looked like their victory was just moments away. However, we know something they didn't, and that is that it wasn't a nine-foot-nine giant and his armor bearer versus a shepherd boy fighting solo. It was a nine foot nine giant and his armor bearer versus a shepherd boy with the God of Israel at his side.

David wasn't alone. He didn't have to be a giant, because his God was great. I think David's audacity is best summed up in a quote by former Scottish minister and reformer William Blaikie, who said, "A man of less faith might have been too nervous to take the proper aim."[4]

David had bold faith, and he was confident that his God was on his side. A lot of times we get a superhero complex. We read stories like this and insert ourselves into the character of David. We think we have to muster up the strength to be a solo fighter in the army of God. But in reality, David isn't the hero of the story. God is. David didn't have to have the courage to fight a giant alone; he just needed to throw his faith into the fight.

In the same way, we have to involve God in our fight, because we simply can't win battles on our own.

Look up these Old Testament verses about when Israel went to war. Beside each reference, write what the verse says God will do on their behalf.

- Exodus 14:14

- Deuteronomy 3:22

- Deuteronomy 20:4

- 2 Chronicles 20:17

- Isaiah 54:17

While David was the only Israelite to step into the valley, his brothers were there too, watching. They were soldiers in Saul's army, sitting on that dusty hillside with thousands of other men who would have been cheering for David.

Did you know that the New Testament uses a Greek word that means "one another" or "each other" about one hundred times, and the majority of those mentions are commands for how to relate to others?[5] They say things like "love one another" (John 13:34), "bear with each other" (Col. 3:13), and "honor one another" (Rom. 12:10).

Here's the deal: We cannot "one another" without others. It's clear that God never meant for us to go into life's battles alone. We were always supposed to go with God and our friends by our side, cheering us on and helping us walk in the right direction.

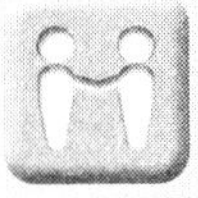

Find Your Friends

Since my friend Kimberly Stuart and I have each written several books, she and I had this crazy thought that we could lock arms with our experience to help other writers turn their book-writing dreams into reality. So we created a podcast called *The Writing Room*. It's a space where we can come alongside fellow writers to cheer them on and give them the nudge they need to overcome whatever giants are in their path that are keeping them from putting onto the page what is in their heart.

I guess I could've done a podcast on my own. But Kimberly's leadership and friendship clearly make our podcast better. Without her, it would just be me blabbing about writing tips or my next zany idea.

What I've found through cohosting a podcast (and from about a million other experiences in my life) is that when we invite others into our fight, we finish stronger, have a greater impact on others, and put a bigger smile on God's face.

Take a moment to reflect:

- **Who can you invite into your fight with you? Write down their names in the space below and seek out time with them. Find out how you can cheer each other on.**

We may not know how to sling a stone at our giants like David did, but we can gather some friends and throw our faith into the fight. Together, we can hurl prayer, wisdom, encouragement, resources, and anything else we have at our giants until they fall. Because eventually, with God on our side, the giants do fall.

- **Even before Goliath fell, David gave an impressive victory speech. Read 1 Samuel 17:45–47 (NASB) and write down David's "so that" statement (v. 46) in the blank below:**

David is quick to point out that this giant will die and the Philistines will fall "so that all the earth may know that there is a God in Israel."

David understood something that would be wise for us to also discover: God doesn't offer us victory so that we can show the world how impressive we are. He conquers His enemies on our behalf so that the world will see how mighty our God is.

As we wrap up our time in the Valley of Elah, ponder what your "so that all the earth may know that there is a God" sentence looks like. Here are some ideas: "I'm going to conquer this addiction ... handle the hits life has thrown at me ... break these generational curses for my children ... love prickly people well in my community ... lead with love ... *so that* all the world will know there is a God."

- **Write your "so that" sentence (or maybe sentences) in the space below:**

Now, let's go find some giants. And then let's knock 'em down—together.

Personal Travel Log

Reach deep. In the Valley of Elah, we learned that David's defeat of Goliath wasn't just one of the most epic underdog victories in history but also a blueprint for how Christians can conquer the giants in their own lives. We've asked ourselves what it means to trust God not just for the courage to fight but also for victory as He fights with us and for us.

David's confidence wasn't in his sling skills but in his Savior. He didn't even wear Saul's armor or fight like the other warriors around him. Likewise, God equips us with our own unique skill set to fight life's battles. Our pain and past experiences are actually tools God uses for breakthrough.

As we step out into our own valleys to face giants, we can know we are never alone. God is with us. We have fellow fighters cheering us on. As we see victories in our lives and in the lives of others, it's not so we can boast; it's so we can point people to the greatness of our God. Every victory is a testimony.

God is sending us from the Valley of Elah, asking us to allow Him to fight on our behalf as we throw everything we've got at the giants in our lives. The Great Defender is on our side.

As you reflect on what you just learned, answer these questions:

- **What is your key takeaway from this section?**

- **Where do you see God at work in your life and in the lives of others around you?**

- **What is God calling you to do in light of our time in the Valley of Elah?**

- **What direction do you think He wants you to go next?**

Pray

God,

We're stepping into the valley to face our giants with a little bit of courage and fear. But we're showing up with all our weaknesses and strengths, knowing we don't have to be the strongest or bravest, because You are.

David didn't bring armor and a sword into his fight with Goliath, but he did bring a sling, a few stones, and a heart full of faith. That's what we want too—to trust that You have purposefully given us our gifts and skills.

You've already equipped us to take down giants. We've learned so much through hardship and in the quiet places. If You can use a slingshot to drop a nine-foot-nine giant, what more could You do when we trust You with what You have placed in our hands?

Lord, please send us some people, fellow fighters, who won't stay on the sidelines of the battle but will run alongside us—friends who will pray boldly, cheer hard, and speak the truth when the giants' lies get loud.

When the giants fall and we see victory on the other side of life's battles, help us remember that this was all about You. It always has been. May our lives shout to the world, "There is a God in this valley, and He's not done yet."

Amen.

Extend Your Stay

If you want to spend a little more time at this stop, scan the QR code here (access code: Journey). You can take a tour through the Valley of Elah, download a digital recipe, and find cool links.

Recipe

Labneh

Before David was a giant slayer, he was a cheese-snacking shepherd. I'm kidding. I don't know the cheese part for sure. But it's possible that before he squared up with Goliath, he was eating some labneh.

The Valley of Elah is in southern Israel, where this creamy, tangy, strained yogurt cheese is very popular. It was even a main food among the ancient Philistine and Israelite people groups who resided in this area. Think of it as cream cheese with a swagger.

Unfortunately, I couldn't bring you a giant and sling today to tell you about David and Goliath, but I can offer you a recipe to experience a taste of the land where this great historical event went down.

Labneh is simple. It's creamy. It's spreadable. And when you drizzle olive oil on it and sprinkle it with za'atar, it's basically holy ground on a pita.

So here's what I want you to do: Take a bite and remember: God loves using simple things. A stone. A shepherd. A snack. Maybe even you. Let's taste and see that the Lord is good—and that labneh isn't so bad either.

YOU WILL NEED:

2 cups full-fat plain Greek yogurt
½ teaspoon salt
Olive oil, for drizzling
Za'atar seasoning (Middle Eastern herb blend)
Pita bread or naan, for dipping

DIRECTIONS:

1. Mix the yogurt and salt in a bowl.

2. Spoon it into a cheesecloth-lined strainer over another bowl. Let it drain in the refrigerator for 12–24 hours until thick like cream cheese.
3. Scoop into a dish, drizzle generously with olive oil, and sprinkle with za'atar.
4. Serve with warm pita or fresh veggies. Enjoy with your friends!

The Sea of Galilee

STOP 8

RUNNING WITH DELIGHT AT THE SEA OF GALILEE

Bob's Travel Log

I'm back here on the Sea of Galilee, right where it all started. Standing on the shore where Jesus first called His disciples, inhaling the salt air and the scent of olive trees, I can't help but wonder if I would have been bold and curious enough to have dropped my net and gone after Jesus to become a "fisher of men."

After just three years of walking with Jesus along this beach, through many towns, in all kinds of wild situations, these men who said yes to Jesus saw Him crucified and then raised to life. When the chips were down, Peter, one of Jesus' loudest, boldest, and most loyal disciples, messed up big. He denounced Jesus—not just once but three times, even claiming not to know Him.

But Jesus didn't cancel Peter. He cooked for him. Right here on this beach.

After all the drama of the trial, crucifixion, and resurrection, the disciples went back to fishing—maybe because they didn't know what else to do. We all revert to our old ways from time to time. The resurrected Jesus shouted from the shore, "Throw your net on the right side of the boat" (John 21:6). Peter recognized *that* voice. Without hesitation, like kids whose parents have just called them inside for cake, Peter cannonballed into the water and swam toward Jesus.

What did Jesus do? He made breakfast. He offered them bread and fish—and forgiveness.

This place reminds me that God's not interested in our résumés or regrets: He's after our hearts. He's forever pulling up a chair for us at His table and asking us to commune and be with Him, dressed just as we are.

Like the disciples who heard Jesus call them from the shoreline, I want to listen for the truest voice. My ears are tuned in to Jesus' voice, which doesn't shout us down for our mistakes but calls us close.

I press my feet into the sand and incline my ear toward the ocean, trying to listen better. Because if I hear Jesus' voice above this noisy world, I know that's the only voice worth running toward for the rest of my life.

It's time to watch the video for this stop.
Settle in for a few minutes and scan the QR code (access code: Journey).

Drop a Pin

- **Where are you right now in relation to what I spoke about in this section's video? Excited? Curious? Lost? Jot down your thoughts in the space below.**

RUNNING TOWARD JESUS AT THE SEA OF GALILEE

Read Your Map

Afterward Jesus appeared again to his disciples, by the Sea of Galilee. It happened this way: Simon Peter, Thomas (also known as Didymus), Nathanael from Cana in Galilee, the sons of Zebedee, and two other disciples were together. "I'm going out to fish," Simon Peter told them, and they said, "We'll go with you." So they went out and got into the boat, but that night they caught nothing.

Early in the morning, Jesus stood on the shore, but the disciples did not realize that it was Jesus.

He called out to them, "Friends, haven't you any fish?"

"No," they answered.

He said, "Throw your net on the right side of the boat and you will find some." When they did, they were unable to haul the net in because of the large number of fish.

Then the disciple whom Jesus loved said to Peter, "It is the Lord!" As soon as Simon Peter heard him say, "It is the Lord," he wrapped his outer garment around him (for he had taken it off) and jumped into the water. The other disciples followed in the boat, towing the net full of fish, for they were not far from shore, about a hundred yards. When they landed, they saw a fire of burning coals there with fish on it, and some bread.

Jesus said to them, "Bring some of the fish you have just caught." So Simon Peter climbed back into the boat and dragged the net ashore. It was full of large fish, 153, but even with so many the net was not torn. Jesus said to them, "Come and have breakfast." None of the disciples dared ask him, "Who are you?" They knew it was the Lord. Jesus came, took the bread and gave it to them, and did the same with the fish. This was now the third time Jesus appeared to his disciples after he was raised from the dead. (John 21:1–14)

Group Discussion Prompt

Going back isn't always going backward.

In all my years working with people, I've discovered that sometimes we return to old dreams, places, or patterns because we want to see how much we've grown. For example, sometimes I'll revisit a place that used to hold significance in my life to reminisce but to also celebrate all that's happened in the time I've been away. Or I'll pick up an old hobby to see if I'm better at it now that I'm older and wiser.

Sometimes we have to circle back to what we once loved to get closure on the question: Is this something I need to walk away from completely, or am I being invited to walk back into this with a new heart?

We can only speculate, but I think this is more or less what Peter was doing when he declared, "I'm going fishing." He might have been wondering if God was sending him back to the Sea of Galilee to be a fisherman after being a fisher of men. Or maybe he thought he deserved to go backward because of his mistakes.

- Have you ever gone back to "fishing" after you failed God? Why do you think we tend to revert to our old ways when we're unsure what to do?

- What's good about going back? What isn't so great?

If you were counting, in this Scripture, Peter and six other disciples decided to go on a fishing trip on the Sea of Galilee. It sounds like a lighthearted, fun outing until you know the significance of this shore and sea for these men.

- **Read Matthew 4:18–22. Compare these verses and John 21:1–14. What is the same? What's different? What do you notice?**

About three years have passed between Matthew 4 and John 12, and we see Peter coming back full circle to being a fisherman. Some scholars believe that Peter was being disobedient to his call to be a "fisher of men" by hopping in the boat and picking up a net again. Some think he needed to clear his head, and a night of fishing was how he'd always done that in the past. Others think he was just doing the only thing he knew to do, which might not necessarily have been a bad thing. When you're uncertain about life, going back to the last thing God had you doing is a pretty good strategy.

We don't know quite what Peter was up to or why, but we know that Jesus had once called these men (some of whom had been fishermen) to be fishers of men. And then, after His resurrection, He returned to the Sea of Galilee to visit these same men on the same shore to call out to them in the same voice.

Despite so many similarities, the disciples don't seem to have recognized Jesus immediately, which speaks to the unexpected way Jesus always seemed to appear in their lives. He was constantly catching them off guard in their old ways and pointing them toward something new.

- **Let's flip back to the Old Testament and review a prophecy about Jesus in Isaiah 43:19. What did it say God was doing and would do?**

- **How was Jesus the "new thing" and "way" God's people were longing for?**

Jesus asked these men to do something new when He told them to throw the net on the other side of the boat. After catching nothing all night long, they changed their strategy according to Jesus' direction and—*bam!*—there were more fish than their nets should have been able to carry. The difference wasn't their fishing method: It was that they were following Jesus. Jesus' way is always more effective.

- **Jump to Luke 5:1–11. This is another account of the moment when Jesus first called Peter (a.k.a. Simon or Simon Peter in this passage) to follow Him. What happened?**

- **How was this similar to what occurred in John 21?**

When the disciples witnessed the astounding number of fish in their nets, everything changed. They had seen this before. The familiar way their obedience led to a miraculous catch of fish allowed the disciples to finally recognize the resurrected Jesus.

- **For Peter, the boat couldn't move fast enough, so he jumped into the water and swam to his Lord, teacher, and friend. Take a moment to glance back at a moment Peter had already shared with Jesus on the water in Matthew 14:25–33. What did Peter do?**

Maybe Peter thought if he jumped out of the boat this time, he'd be able to run on the sea all the way to shore. Jesus and Peter always seemed to have remarkable encounters at the water, and this one was no different.

Take a moment to compare these two verses about the miracles that occurred first at Peter's calling and then again at his calling *back* to Jesus by filling in the blanks:

> When they had done so, they caught such a large number of fish that their nets began to ______________________." (Luke 5:6)

> Jesus said to them, "Bring some of the fish you have just caught." So Simon Peter climbed back into the boat and dragged the net ashore. It was full of large fish, 153, but even with so many the net was ______________________. (John 21:10–11)

Before we wrap up the spiritual significance of this, we need to note that Peter lugged that net ashore with 153 fish. A waterlogged fisherman's net plus that many fish would have weighed up to three hundred pounds.[1] Peter was a strong guy! If Jesus asked me to do that, I'd have to start praying for supernatural strength.

But Jesus knew Peter's strength. And remember, the first time Peter witnessed a miracle just like this (see Luke 5:1–11), the net began to tear. The net's durability this time could have been to show the disciples how strong Jesus was. For this new era, He needed them to trust and lean on His teachings and the Holy Spirit to carry them through. He required them to continue to be fishers of men as they would soon begin to share the gospel with the world. Just like their net carried those fish, Jesus' presence and the Holy Spirit would be strong enough to carry them through this next season of starting churches and preaching the message of Christ.

When Peter got the net to shore, Jesus invited the disciples to "come and have breakfast" (John 21:12). Jesus offered several invitations throughout the New Testament. Look up the following verses and write down the "come and" statement Jesus made in each.

- Matthew 11:28–29

- Matthew 25:34–36

- Mark 6:31

- John 1:39

Jesus loves inviting us in. We're all welcome at His table. So pause a moment and listen to Jesus' voice. Hear Him invite you into all the joy, purpose, grace, and forgiveness He has to offer. He's casting His net wide, and He's stronger than we could ever understand, with arms big enough to hold us all.

Like Peter, may we cannonball into all that God has for us, knowing that even when our past has left us with uncertainties and hardship, wild and wonderful things are ahead.

Drop a Pin

- **Of the "come and" invitations that Jesus made in the New Testament, which one resonates the most with you right now? Why is that? Take a moment to pray, reflect, and write down what invitation you think Jesus is specifically extending to you in this era of your life.**

THE GOD OF SECOND CHANCES

Read Your Map

> When they had finished eating, Jesus said to Simon Peter, "Simon son of John, do you love me more than these?"
>
> "Yes, Lord," he said, "you know that I love you."
>
> Jesus said, "Feed my lambs."
>
> Again Jesus said, "Simon son of John, do you love me?"
>
> He answered, "Yes, Lord, you know that I love you."
>
> Jesus said, "Take care of my sheep."
>
> The third time he said to him, "Simon son of John, do you love me?"
>
> Peter was hurt because Jesus asked him the third time, "Do you love me?" He said, "Lord, you know all things; you know that I love you."
>
> Jesus said, "Feed my sheep." (John 21:15–17)

After a very wet Peter had made his way to land, I wonder if he knelt to warm himself by the fire Jesus was cooking breakfast on.

And that makes me wonder if Peter looked at the hot coals and recalled the night when he was warming himself by another fire.

- **Read Luke 22:55–62. What did Peter do by a fire that may have caused guilt or shame when it came to his relationship with Jesus?**

Peter loved Jesus deeply, yet he had denied a connection with his Savior three times. I can't imagine the weight of shame or regret he carried because of this.

- **But look at what Jesus did for Peter over breakfast in John 21:15–17. What did Jesus ask Peter? How did he respond? How many questions did Jesus ask him?**

Group Discussion Prompt

Throughout the New Testament, we see that Jesus' main teaching tactic was to ask questions. In the four Gospels (Matthew, Mark, Luke, and John) alone, Jesus asks over three hundred questions.[2]

- Why do you think Jesus asked Peter these questions?
- Sometimes we all need to be reminded of our identity and pointed back toward our mission. How have you seen this play out in modern times within your church, community, or personal life?

Peter denied Jesus three times at the illegal trial held by the Jewish religious leaders the night before His crucifixion. Then, after Jesus had died and risen again, Jesus asked Peter three questions ... three chances to restore Peter's reputation as a disciple in front of the other disciples. Instead of publicly scolding Peter for his betrayal, Jesus showered him with grace and restored him. He invited Peter back in.

There's something inside us that longs for purpose, direction, and acceptance. Deep down, Jesus knew the answers to the questions He was asking Peter. He just needed Peter to declare his devotion out loud. Really, it was Peter who needed to declare it out loud. He needed to hear himself say the words, and the others needed to hear them, as well.

We too need to tell Jesus we love Him and get active about sharing that love with others. Sometimes we just need to know that we can begin again—especially if we, like Peter, have answered those questions wrong before. It's essential to know that we're allowed to keep trying.

Look at the following verses written by Peter himself about how God can divinely reset our lives. Summarize Peter's words in the spaces below.

- 1 Peter 4:12–13

- 1 Peter 5:10

We all make mistakes, and we all go through hard stuff. Peter reminds us that, when we mess up, Jesus can restore not only our mission but also our identity.

Find Your Friends

I think it's really great that after Peter jumped into the water, the other disciples followed him (in the boat). They helped haul in the fish. They also sat down with Jesus for breakfast. Now, they could have seen Peter go overboard and thought, *Oh, Crazy Pete is at it again.* They also could've shown that they no longer considered him their leader, maybe by not following his lead. But they went with him and remained together.

We all need friends like that—people who go with us as we try to move toward Jesus, remind us of who we're becoming, and speak over us with voices of truth and love. Because the harsh reality is that what the people we love the most say about us has an influence on who we become. In Christ, we are not powerless. We don't have to conform to what others say about us. But their words still have an impact.

If I'm honest, sometimes I forget who I am. Not like I don't remember that my name is Bob (anyone could remember that!). More like, when I fail, I can start to think I'm a failure. When I'm insecure, I lose the bravery and boldness to show up the way God created me to. So I keep a group of close friends on speed dial who I know will remind me of my calling when I get distracted or discouraged. They don't just cheer me on; they also challenge me. When I need to hear it, they state, "Bob, this is not you. You are not this kind of guy. Stop acting like this."

What about you? How can you be a voice that echoes Jesus' love back to others? Who should you put on your speed dial list to remind you of the truth about who God created you to be?

Let's face it: We don't need friends who keep score. We get enough of that on social media and experience enough of the comparison and production game at work. We need friends who remind us that we are beloved, friends who tell us, "You're still invited to Jesus' table. God loves you a whole, whole lot."

Our God is a God of second chances. He never gives up on us and is always inviting us back. We can cannonball into His grace and mercy at any time. The next time we think our mess-ups or sins have disqualified us from His table, we can remember standing on this shoreline at the Sea of Galilee. We can picture Peter with tears in his eyes as he declared that he did indeed love Jesus. We too can know what it feels like to renew our own relationship with God.

Even our greatest setbacks can become setups for a future full of hope if we're willing to drop our shame, face Jesus, and find our identity in Him.

Drop a Pin

- **Imagine sitting and talking with Jesus over breakfast on the shore of the Sea of Galilee. If He turned to you and asked, "Do you love me?" what would you say?**

- **If He told you to go and feed his sheep, meaning to love and serve others, what action steps would you take? How can you incorporate these steps into your daily life?**

LISTEN FOR THE VOICE YOU TRUST

Read Your Map

> "Very truly I tell you, when you were younger you dressed yourself and went where you wanted; but when you are old you will stretch out your hands, and someone else will dress you and lead you where you do not want to go." Jesus said this to indicate the kind of death by which Peter would glorify God. Then he said to him, "Follow me!"
>
> Peter turned and saw that the disciple whom Jesus loved was following them. (This was the one who had leaned back against Jesus at the supper and had said, "Lord, who is going to betray you?") When Peter saw him, he asked, "Lord, what about him?"
>
> Jesus answered, "If I want him to remain alive until I return, what is that to you? You must follow me." Because of this, the rumor spread among the believers that this disciple would not die. But Jesus did not say that he would not die; he only said, "If I want him to remain alive until I return, what is that to you?"
>
> This is the disciple who testifies to these things and who wrote them down. We know that his testimony is true.
>
> Jesus did many other things as well. If every one of them were written down, I suppose that even the whole world would not have room for the books that would be written. (John 21:18–25)

The world sure is full of distractions, isn't it? We've got music blaring in our cars, TVs gibbering in our homes, and entertainment and information constantly streaming on our phones. If you're a parent or grandparent like me with young children running around, there is laughter and shouting, toys clanging together as they fall out of bins, and the pitter-patter of little feet running all over the place. Silence and focus can be a bit hard to come by these days. And if we're not careful, we can allow ourselves to be surrounded by so many distractions, even beautiful distractions like grandchildren, that we miss the voice of God.

Something happened after Peter confessed his love for Jesus and received his mission. Jesus concluded their conversation with an ominous statement. He told Peter how he was going to die. He would again encounter a cross, but this time he would be on it. In his death, he would glorify God.

In his commentary, Adam Clarke states that "about thirty-four years after this, Peter was crucified; and that he deemed it so *glorious* a thing to die for Christ that he begged to be crucified with his *head downwards*, not considering himself worthy to die in the same posture in which his Lord did."[3]

How incredible is that? Can you imagine Jesus telling you how it's all going to end? That would throw me for a loop. But, in true Peter-like fashion, he seemed almost reassured by this. He was ready to accept the challenge to spend—and end—his life glorifying God, even if it meant carrying his own cross.

Peter was reinstated by Jesus, given a call to "feed the sheep," and even told he was going to die glorifying God. What's interesting is that Peter's response wasn't to take a walk down the shore to ponder all this and let it sink in. He didn't need to go out fishing again to clear his head. He didn't say a prayer or hug Jesus. He noticed John following them (see John 21:20–21) and immediately got distracted. He asked Jesus, "What about that guy?"

Peter is all of us. We have this great tendency to receive from God and then get so distracted by what other people are doing. We feel ready to start that new job, send that text to invite over a friend, or get dressed to head out the door to church. We're all good until we hop on social media and second-guess if we're really cut out for our job because others look more successful than we are. Someone has more friends than we do. Somebody's church outfit is way better than ours. All of a sudden, we're wondering, *What about them?*

- **Do you ever find yourself doing this? What's been distracting for you lately?**

When Jesus answered Peter, "If I want him to remain alive until I return, what is that to you? You must follow me" (v. 22), He was letting Peter in on the fact that John's mission wasn't Peter's

Group Discussion Prompt

We've made it through a whole Bible study together, so I think I can be honest with you: Sometimes I think I have "shiny syndrome." A fun opportunity pops up, I get a new idea, I see what someone else is doing over there, and I think, *Hmm, let's try that.* But in reality, I haven't finished the work in front of me. God has given me a mission that I haven't completed. I'm not yet free to chase after something new and shiny.

So I have to refocus. Jesus said, "Follow Me this way," which means I need to follow Him in that way, not some other way. It reminds me that I'm not ready to head in another direction yet.

Trust me. I've had to learn the hard way. I've spent entire seasons distracted by fear, insecurities, performance, and a longing to be impressive. What I've learned is that we all get distracted. Shiny stuff pops up in all our paths. But it's up to us to look back at Jesus and say, "Oh, yeah ... I'm not going that way. I'm going Your way."

- Why do you think it's so easy for us to get distracted?
- How do we know what direction Jesus wants us to walk?
- What does focusing on and following Jesus look like for you?

mission. Everyone's journey looks different. Jesus' second invitation for Peter to follow Him called him back into focus. Because of the way Jesus answered Peter's question about John's future, a rumor spread among the early Christians that John was essentially going to live forever. But even in that, Jesus still asked Peter to drown out the noise and focus on His call on Peter's life.

Look up Hebrews 12:1–2 and John 10:27 and fill in the blanks:

Therefore, since we are surrounded by such a great cloud of witnesses, let us throw off _____ ______________________________________ ______________________________ and the sin that so easily entangles. And let us run with perseverance the race marked out for us, fixing our eyes on ______________________, the pioneer and perfecter of faith. For the joy set before him he endured the cross, scorning its shame, and sat down at the right hand of the throne of God.

My sheep listen to my ___________________; I _______________________ them, and they _________________________ me.

The world and all its distractions seem to yell at us, but Jesus gently calls. He doesn't shout us down; He draws us in.

The Sea of Galilee was smaller than I thought it would be. I have spent a lot of my time in California gazing at the grand Pacific Ocean. When I hear the word *sea*, I think of vast expanses of rolling water with surfers and seagulls. However, the Sea of Galilee is only sixty-four square miles. It's more like a big lake.

Isn't it super interesting that Jesus chose this small body of water as the place to call disciples, calm a storm, cast out demons, and spend most of His time?

- **Jesus wasn't into shiny, flashy things. Take a look at Matthew 8:20. What does it say that Jesus didn't have?**

Jesus was simple, poor by worldly standards. He was always drawn to secret places, and He used ordinary people to do extraordinary things. Living like this would have eliminated a lot of distraction.

While we can't all enjoy a getaway at a rustic, peaceful seashore, we can all find a secret place where we can get quiet and hear the voice of God.

- **Read Psalm 91, and write down in your own words what is offered by God in the secret place:**

When we get away from all the noise and sit in God's presence, we realize that the world yells but Jesus calls us in. He gently asks us, as He did Peter, to follow Him. He doesn't scream His invitation at us or cram it down our throats. But if we have "shiny syndrome," we may miss it because we're too busy noticing what everyone else is doing. When we're looking all around for purpose, we don't notice Jesus stepping out in front to show us the way.

So, as we wrap up our trip through the Holy Land together, let's walk how Love walked. Slowly. Carefully. Intentionally. Listening to His Father's voice. Going out on mission where God told Him to go. Take a while to sit on this shoreline, listen to the wind and the waves, and ask Jesus to speak. See if you can pick up God's voice calling, "My son, My daughter, come and follow Me."

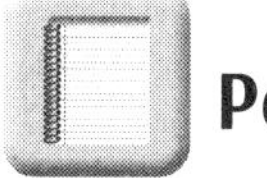

Personal Travel Log

Reach deep. Here at the Sea of Galilee, we've walked the shore where Jesus first called the disciples and then called them back to Him again. We've learned that Jesus isn't keeping score; He's actually setting a place for us at His table.

We've identified with Peter both when he made some great mistakes and when he went back to his old hobbies. Maybe he felt too far gone, but possibly he just didn't know what else to do. Have you ever been there? Have you jumped back into an old routine and wondered if your part to play in God's story was over? But Jesus always shows up, doesn't He? He invites us back again and again because He is the God of second chances, calling us over for breakfast even when we've sailed away from Him.

Like Peter, may we jump out of the boat of our comfort zone and cannonball back into God's grace, where He offers a future full of purpose and hope in Jesus. May we learn to recognize the voice of our Savior. May we focus on Him despite all the distractions of the world, as He reminds us of our calling to love God and love people.

Whether we're still in the boat, swimming toward Jesus, or distracted by what everyone else is doing, the call is still the same: "Follow Me."

In light of what we just learned, consider these questions:

- **What is your key takeaway from this section?**

- **Where do you see God at work in your life and in the lives of others around you?**

- **What is God calling you to do after our time at the Sea of Galilee?**

- **What direction do you think He wants you to go next?**

Pray

Jesus,

Thank You for meeting us back where it all started. May we pause and remember what it was like to first hear You call us. Maybe we could hear our name. Or maybe Your call was a prick in our heart we couldn't deny. We're so grateful that You have called us and keep calling us back.

We admit that we get lost sometimes. When life throws us a curveball, we can forget who we are and whose we are. We can get distracted by all the noise of this world and start comparing ourselves to others. Thank You that You don't shame us. You gently remind us that all we need to do is follow You.

Today, we wish to hear Your voice again. Like Peter, may we jump right in and move toward You. We want to follow You more than we have been following the fear, shame, or noise around us.

Help us to get quiet and listen for Your voice, the one that calls us beloved. Help us to love Your people and remember that our failure never gets the last word—You do.

Thank You for second chances, for calling us close even when we've blown it.

We love You and want to follow You ... all the way to the shore and beyond.

Amen.

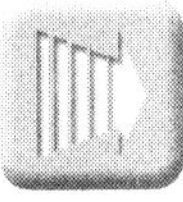

Extend Your Stay

If you want to spend a little more time at this stop, scan the QR code here (access code: Journey). You can take a tour through the Sea of Galilee, download a digital recipe, and find cool links.

Recipe

Shakshuka Breakfast on the Beach

We're going to end this Bible study the same way the book of John ends: with breakfast.

While Jesus and Peter ate fish for breakfast, this particular Galilean breakfast plate is what you might find today if you pulled up a chair in a guesthouse overlooking the Sea of Galilee.

Shakshuka sounds fancy, but it's simply eggs in a tomato-and-pepper sauce. It's a savory and delicious breakfast staple across this region. Traditionally, this meal is eaten straight from the skillet with friends gathered around, dipping bread into the sauce.

As you eat, put yourself in Peter's sandals. Imagine looking up and seeing Jesus making you breakfast on the beach. You're in deep astonishment as you look at Him, since not too many days ago, you saw Him crucified and buried. And yet here He stands. You want to drop to your knees and worship Him. But you're held back because of your shame. The risen Lord has decided to show up after the biggest personal failure of your life.

Yet here He stands, making you breakfast. He comes to you, loves you, and cares for you, exactly where you are.

Let's eat like we're with Jesus on the beach. In our final stop on our Bible study trip together, I know that God is already cooking something up just for you.

YOU WILL NEED:

1 tablespoon olive oil
1 small onion, diced
1 red bell pepper, diced
2 garlic cloves, minced
1 teaspoon paprika
½ teaspoon cumin
1 14-ounce can diced tomatoes
4 eggs

Chopped parsley or cilantro, for garnish

Bread and jam, olives, or fruit, for serving (optional)

DIRECTIONS:

1. In a skillet over medium heat, heat the olive oil. Sauté the onion and pepper until soft.
2. Add garlic, paprika, and cumin and stir for 30 seconds.
3. Add tomatoes, season with salt and pepper, and simmer for 10–15 minutes.
4. Make 4 wells in the sauce, and crack one egg into each well. Cover and cook until the whites are set.
5. Garnish with herbs, and serve straight from the pan with fresh bread and jam, olives, fruit, and juice or mint tea.

Multiply this recipe as needed for the size of your group. Have fun dipping together!*

*Based on a recipe from www.themediterraneandish.com/shakshuka-recipe.

CONCLUSION

Walking How Love Walked from the Holy Land to Home

You can't go anywhere in the Holy Land without bumping into an olive tree. Seriously, they're everywhere—roots sprawled out like they own the place, trunks twisting like a dance move from someone who's been at it for a few thousand years. Some are just beginning to grow. Others might've been tiny sprouts back when Jesus was walking by. Isn't that something?

When we think about what it means to walk the way Love walked—and still walks—we can think of those olive trees. Here are some aspects of olive trees that are worth pondering:

Olive tree roots are wide.

> So that Christ may dwell in your hearts through faith. And I pray that you, being rooted and established in love, may have power, together with all the Lord's holy people, to grasp how wide and long and high and deep is the love of Christ. (Eph. 3:17–18)

Throughout this study, we saw Jesus heal the outcasts and call the disciples. Peter had a vision from God that revealed that all were invited to His table. This is what love does: It opens its arms wide and makes room. We should too. Our time of pulling up chairs to God's table doesn't have to end here in the Holy Land. At home, let's love people big by letting our roots stretch so wide that people are drawn in and get all tangled up in the grace and purpose of God's love too.

The olive fruit is pressed.

> We are hard pressed on every side, but not crushed; perplexed, but not in despair; persecuted, but not abandoned; struck down, but not destroyed. We always carry around in our body the death of Jesus, so that the life of Jesus may also be revealed in our body. (2 Cor. 4:8–10)

Olive oil is a staple throughout the world. It's made by squashing the olive. After our time on this journey, we will encounter moments where we too are pressed. We will all, unfortunately, encounter a valley of the shadow of death at home. We'll face giants. We will be hit by the storms of life. But we can remember that something valuable—the oil, anointing, and fragrance of a life poured out for others—comes from those pressing times. God is bringing new oil out of us when we feel like we're being squished and squashed from all sides.

Don't get discouraged in the pressing. Love is walking with you and drawing something good out of you. Because of that, you can always take steps forward toward victory.

Olive oil was used for anointing.

> But you have an anointing from the Holy One, and all of you know the truth. (1 John 2:20)

Throughout biblical times, olive oil was poured over people's heads to signify that they were marked by God, had a special calling, and were blessed. Through Mary of Magdala, Paul, and the crazy faith of disciples and friends, we know that we too carry a special anointing because of what Jesus has done in our lives. We can bring to Jesus a friend who needs healing, access the Creator of the universe with just a prayer, and live our lives set apart as members of the upside-down kingdom of God. What a great mystery it is to be a child of God! What a wild, whimsical, heaven-sized mystery that we get to keep learning more and more about for the rest of our lives.

As we head home, let's take the Holy Land with us. We can even grab a real olive tree to grow in our kitchen window or outside in our backyard to remind us ...

We have deep roots. We've been through some pressing and have made it out to the other side, and now we have pure oil to pour out.

We are loved. Let's walk like it. Talk like it. Live like people who belong at God's table—and who are making room for a lot more chairs.

The olive tree is never finished growing, and neither are we.

Let's keep walking. Love's already gone ahead of us.

ACKNOWLEDGMENTS

The Holy Land is a complicated place, full of tribes, generations, and people. This book is a reflection of the same truth shaped in ancient Palestine. The Holy Land is not about any one individual and what they accomplished but of many faithful people who did their part with their eyes fixed on God as they pursued a worthwhile purpose.

Thank you to Sweet Maria and the rest of Team Goff for letting me go missing on so many trips to the Holy Land to film this project. I want to thank the many people with the David C Cook team who made this work possible. First, to Kaley Rivera Thompson, who gave life to these words and daily reflections: Well done and thank you. A massive thank-you also to Michael Covington, Stephanie Bennett, Judy Gillispie, James Hershberger, Leah Von Fange, Gabe Wicks, Rudy Kish, Jeff Gerke, Annette Brickbealer, and Rob Annese. Your legacy is going to be your love, released into the world through the excellence of your work and compassion for people.

I also want to thank our film crew and host team who traveled together, ate together, and got lost and found together. First of all, thank you to Emily Vogeltanz, who was our fearless leader, visionary, queen of kindness, and vault of knowledge. Thank you to Matthew Garvin, our videographer, and Tairo Arrabal, who did our sound engineering and spent countless hours holding a long boom microphone. Thank you also to the amazing team at Keshet Journeys, led by my friend Moshe Gabay and assisted by a great team including Pascal Scheidegger, who helped with logistics and permits, and Ashraf, my friend and our fearless driver.

Finally, I want to thank the Love Does team, led by Jody Luke, and my personal team in San Diego, who worked tirelessly and looked after every detail to make this work possible. Thank you, Stephanie Wesson, for seeing this from beginning to end and tending to every detail. Katie Orr, thank you for all the logistics of getting people where they needed to be, including me. You both are love's heroes and work tirelessly for the benefit of others.

If you enjoy this project as much as I have enjoyed working alongside all these people, this work will have indeed been a huge success.

Bob

NOTES

Stop 1

1. "Easton's Bible Dictionary—Capernaum," Bible Study Tools, accessed September 15, 2025, www.biblestudytools.com/dictionary/Capernaum.

Stop 3

1. "Magdala," Jewish Virtual Library, American-Israeli Cooperative Enterprise, accessed August 4, 2025, www.jewishvirtuallibrary.org/magdala.

2. "Of Magdala," *50 Days: Celebrating the Easter Season* (blog), Forward Movement, April 29, 2023, https://50days.org/2023/04/of-magdala.

3. "Duc in Altum," Magdala, accessed August 4, 2025, www.magdala.org/duc-in-altum.

4. "Duc in Altum."

5. Cristobal Vilaroig, "A Franciscan Describing Towers," Magdala, January 19, 2023, www.magdala.org/journal/history-a-franciscan-describing-towers#article.

6. Bob Goff, *Everybody, Always: Becoming Love in a World Full of Setbacks and Difficult People* (Nelson Books, 2018), 148.

7. Biblical Archaeology Society Staff, "BAR Test Kitchen," Biblical Archaeology Society, September 4, 2018, www.biblicalarchaeology.org/daily/ancient-cultures/daily-life-and-practice/bar-test-kitchen-ancient-recipes.

Stop 6

1. "Matthew 5—the Sermon on the Mount," Enduring Word, accessed August 4, 2025, https://enduringword.com/bible-commentary/matthew-5.

2. "Bob Goff: Finding Hope Through Hardship," *Relevant*, December 11, 2024, https://relevantmagazine.com/culture/bob-goff-finding-hope-through-hardship.

3. "Understanding Disorders: What Are Anxiety and Depression?," Anxiety & Depression Association of America, accessed August 4, 2025, http://adaa.org/understanding-anxiety.

Stop 7

1. "David Defeats Goliath of Gath," The Bible Journey, accessed August 4, 2025, www.thebiblejourney.org/biblejourney2/30-israel-becomes-a-kingdom-under-saul-and-david/david-defeats-goliath-of-gath.

2. "Valley of Elah: David and Goliath," Holy Land Site, accessed August 4, 2025, www.holylandsite.com/valley-of-elah.

3. Michael Griego, "Number 40 in the Bible," Biblical Viewpoint, May 3, 2024, https://biblicalviewpoint.com/2024/05/03/number-40-in-the-bible.

4. "First Samuel 17:32–37, 42–50 Notes," ChurchBibleStudies.org, accessed August 4, 2025, www.churchbiblestudies.org/first-samuel-17-32-37-42-50-notes.

5. Peter Krol, "4 Tips for Reading the One Anothers in the Bible," Word by Word, Logos Bible Study App, August 15, 2023, www.logos.com/grow/min-one-anothers.

Stop 8

1. "John 21—the Restoration of Peter," Enduring Word, accessed August 4, 2025, https://enduringword.com/bible-commentary/john-21.

2. Bob Tiede, "Why Did Jesus Ask So Many Questions?," Biblical Leadership, January 24, 2020, www.biblicalleadership.com/blogs/why-did-jesus-ask-so-many-questions.

3. Adam Clarke, *Clarke's Commentary: Matthew–Revelation* (Abingdon, 1977), italics in the original.

ANSWER KEY (from p. 41)

- Betrayed by his son (David/Jesus)
- Betrayed by Judas (David/Jesus)
- Prayed on the Mount of Olives in the garden of Gethsemane before his arrest (David/Jesus)
- Prayed on the Mount of Olives as he fled for the wilderness (David/Jesus)
- Returned to Jerusalem as king after winning a great battle (David/Jesus)
- Will one day return as the King of Kings (David/Jesus)
- Trusted God for restoration: "If I find favor in the LORD's eyes …" (David/Jesus)
- Submitted to God's will: "Yet not my will, but yours be done" (David/Jesus)
- Had a great earthly kingdom (David/Jesus)
- Has an eternal kingdom and will reign forever (David/Jesus)

ANSWER KEY (from p. 78)

Verses	Foreshadowing
For God so loved the world that he gave his one and only Son, that whoever believes in him shall not perish but have eternal life. (John 3:16)	Mount Moriah, where Abraham offered Isaac, later became the site of the Temple Mount—the very place where Jesus would later be condemned and sacrificed nearby (Golgotha is within walking distance).
He who did not spare his own Son, but gave him up for us all—how will he not also, along with him, graciously give us all things? (Rom. 8:32)	In writing this verse, Paul used similar language as Genesis 22:12—"You have not withheld from me your son"—to describe God's gift.
Behold! The Lamb of God who takes away the sin of the world! (John 1:29 NKJV)	Though written centuries after Abraham, Isaiah's suffering servant fulfills the picture Abraham had anticipated: a Son who would willingly carry the wood (cross), be bound, and be offered.
By faith Abraham, when God tested him, offered Isaac as a sacrifice.... Abraham reasoned that God could even raise the dead. (Heb. 11:17-19)	This verse reflects on Abraham's faith, seeing it as a herald to resurrection hope—fulfilled in Christ.
Then Solomon began to build the temple of the LORD in Jerusalem on Mount Moriah, where the LORD had appeared to his father David. (2 Chron. 3:1)	Isaac is Abraham's "only son," offered in radical obedience and love—mirroring Jesus as God's only Son. God's act of giving His Son echoes Abraham's willingness to give Isaac. God did not hold back.
The LORD has laid on Him the iniquity of us all.... He was led like a lamb to the slaughter. (Isa. 53:6-7)	Jesus is the Lamb that Abraham believed God would provide, finally revealed.